I0020020

Pragmatic Application of Service Management

The Five Anchor Approach

Second edition

Pragmatic Application of Service Management

The Five Anchor Approach

Second edition

S. D. VAN HOVE, ED.D.
MARK THOMAS, M.S.

IT Governance Publishing

Every possible effort has been made to ensure that the information contained in this book is accurate at the time of going to press and the publisher and the author cannot accept responsibility for any errors or omissions, however caused. Any opinions expressed in this book are those of the author, not the publisher. Websites identified are for reference only, not endorsement and any website visits are at the reader's own risk. No responsibility for loss or damage occasioned to any person acting, or refraining from action, as a result of the material in this publication can be accepted by the publisher or the author.

Apart from any fair dealing for the purposes of research or private study, or criticism or review, as permitted under the Copyright, Designs and Patents Act 1988, this publication may only be reproduced, stored or transmitted, in any form, or by any means, with the prior permission in writing of the publisher or, in the case of reprographic reproduction, in accordance with the terms of licences issued by the Copyright Licensing Agency. Enquiries concerning reproduction outside those terms should be sent to the publisher at the following address:

IT Governance Publishing
IT Governance Limited
Unit 3, Clive Court
Bartholomew's Walk
Cambridgeshire Business Park
Ely
Cambridgeshire
CB7 4EA
United Kingdom
www.itgovernance.co.uk

© S. D. Van Hove and Mark Thomas 2014, 2016

The authors have asserted the rights of the author under the Copyright, Designs and Patents Act, 1988, to be identified as the author of this work.

Copyright © AXELOS Limited 2011

CMMI® is a registered trademark of CMMI Institute

IDEAL(SM) is a service mark of CMMI Institute.

First published in the United Kingdom in 2014 by IT Governance Publishing: ISBN 978-1-84928-514-8

Second edition published in 2016
ISBN: 978-1-84928-875-0

FOREWORD

Most people enjoy eating. Let's be honest, eating is about more than just providing nourishment for our bodies. Eating and sharing a meal with someone else is a social activity. And, the fact is, eating can be a real experience.

Part of that experience is certainly situational. In many homes, the kitchen table is where many good stories are told and where important family conversations occur. Similarly, when it comes to our favourite food, we know where to find the best rendition of it (especially if we can't make the dish ourselves.) The location that makes our favourite recipe becomes our "go-to" restaurant, bistro, or gastropub.

Service Management is a lot like food – it can feed and nourish the organization and it can be a real experience. As the chefs in the Service Management kitchen, Suzanne and Mark served up a great menu for us when they launched the *Pragmatic Approach to Service Management.* The dish was already "good eating," and now they have served up an improved recipe!

For me, the truth is that Service Management would not "taste" the same without the contributions from Suzanne and Mark. They have both been my "go-to" throughout my ITSM career and I am proud to call them not just colleagues, but friends. I have a great admiration and respect for their uncanny (no pun intended) ability to harvest a garden rich in taste and calories and still deliver a healthy meal loaded with flavour. And they've done it again!

Unlike other chefs who tweak our favourite recipes and take away what we loved about them, Suzanne and Mark have enhanced their tasty ingredients by adding a scoop of CMMI-SVC and twice as many "caselets" than were in their first edition. Can you say "Yum?!?"

In an age where disruption is the IT norm, Suzanne and Mark's book is the "go-to" resource for service managers who are trying to digest the rich resources from which we may choose. And like all good meals, I hope you will choose to share it with others and savour every bite.

Bon Appétit!

Jay Stuart
ITIL Expert
ISO/IEC 20000 Consultant/Manager
priSM Fellow

ABOUT THE AUTHORS

Dr Suzanne D. Van Hove owns and manages SED-IT, a small service management consulting and training company. She has worked in multiple professional verticals leading or coaching service management initiatives. She has also written and delivered accredited courseware for ITIL®, ISO/IEC 20000 as well as multiple workshops and seminars, both nationally and internationally. She is the current chair for INCITS GIT1 – the US National Mirror of JTC1/SC40, the Special Committee for Service Management. She also leads the US mirror for JTC1/SC7/WG24. Dr Van Hove is an adjunct professor at Indiana University, Kelley School of Business and has served on the Board of Directors of itSMF USA as the knowledge management director. In recognition of her contributions to the service management community, Dr Van Hove was the 2013 recipient of the itSMF USA Lifetime Achievement Award. An opera aficionado and avid rosebush gardener, Dr Van Hove resides in Louisville, KY, USA.

Mark Thomas is the founder and president of Escoute, LLC, an IT Governance consultancy focusing on helping enterprises achieve benefits realization through risk and resource optimization. As a nationally known ITIL and COBIT® expert with more than 20 years of professional experience, Mark's background spans leadership roles from datacentre chief information officer (CIO) to management and IT consulting. Mark has led large teams in outsourced IT arrangements, conducted project management office (PMO), service management and governance activities for major project teams and managed enterprise applications implementations across multiple industries.

Mark has an array of industry experience in the health care, finance, manufacturing, services, high technology and government verticals. When he's not traveling, Mark lives with his family in the Kansas City, MO area and claims to be a 'certified' barbeque judge in his spare time.

ACKNOWLEDGEMENTS

We would like to thank Eileen Forrester (chief executive officer (CEO), Forrester Leadership Group) and M. Lynn Penn (president, Performance and Methods Consulting) for their invaluable insights and contributions to this version. As author of *CMMI for Services, Guidelines for Superior Service*, Eileen's unique perspective has broadened The Five Anchors into a new dimension. Lynn's auditing and appraisal expertise within multiple frameworks including CMMI-DEV, CMMI-SVC, Agile and Lean Six Sigma among others, ensured the mapping accuracy across all frameworks. Without them, version 2 would not exist.

CONTENTS

Contents

INTRODUCTION

Thanks for picking up this book!

If you are looking for a book to help you "implement" COBIT®, ISO/IEC 20000-1:2011[1], 2011 ITIL®, or CMMI®-SVC V1.3[2], put this book down and go find the actual documentation from COBIT, ISO/IEC 20000, ITIL, or CMMI-SVC. Frankly, this isn't the book for you.

This book addresses how to **use** COBIT, ISO/IEC 20000-1, ITIL and CMMI-SVC **together** to create a stronger and more robust Service Management System (SMS). We recognize there are many service management frameworks, standards and methodologies, including those within project management (PMI®, P30®, PRINCE2®). On purpose, we didn't include every service management framework, standard or methodology, or any of the project management frameworks for two reasons:

1. Project management deals with the planning and execution of a defined, funded and agreed plan of action.

2. We wanted to keep the book relevant to today's interests, hence the inclusion of CMMI-SVC and maintain a best practice format:

   o Simple is effective.

However, we received numerous questions about how to apply these frameworks to the very small enterprise (VSE). Frankly, the frameworks, as written, can be applied to any size or type of organization. However, they are not always easy to consolidate into a manageable activity for the VSE *without help*. *Chapter 3* offers new information about how the VSE can utilize these Service Management frameworks to their benefit.

---

[1] For ease of reading, going forward, we will refer to ISO/IEC 20000-1:2011 as ISO/IEC 20000-1.
[2] The frameworks used in this book are the most current versions available at the time of publication.

This is a book on how to evaluate and assess a situation using the Five Anchor Framework and, based on that assessment, apply the guidance from COBIT, ISO/IEC 20000-1, ITIL and CMMI-SVC to create a comprehensive improvement plan. The original five caselets have been augmented with CMMI-SVC information and we have included an extra five caselets. One of the caselets is completely based in the world of business – we are excited about this caselet as it is evidence that Service Management is not just IT-oriented. The mapping table has been updated to include the CMMI-SVC process areas.

Additionally, there has been global interest in the mapping of Service Management frameworks. Two Technical Reports (ISO/IEC 20000-11:2015 and ISO/IEC 20000-12:2016) map ISO/IEC 20000-1:2011 to ITIL and CMMI-SVC. The third mapping is underway where ISO/IEC 20000-1 is mapped to COBIT 5. These mappings might have different results than the table in the back of this book because our mapping uses the COBIT framework as the core framework for a unidirectional mapping (COBIT to ITIL, ISO/IEC 20000-1, CMMI-SVC).

Use this book to **think differently**, leverage the strengths of COBIT, ISO/IEC 20000-1, ITIL and CMMI-SVC to mitigate the inherent weaknesses in each.

Happy Reading!

Suzanne and Mark

CHAPTER 1: WHY THIS BOOK

As independent consultants, we are constantly asked the same set of questions:

- "Aren't these frameworks for big companies only?"
- "Where do we start? What do we **have** to do?"
- "What do we measure?"
- "Is there a difference between 'prescriptive' and 'suggestive' when it comes to frameworks?"
- "Isn't ITIL (*insert any other service management framework/standard/methodology*[3]) better than COBIT (*insert any other service management framework*)?"
- "ITIL (*insert any other service management framework*) doesn't work. What else ya got?"
- "If we use multiple frameworks, how do we fit them together?"

What consistently surprises us is the prevalent "one service management body of knowledge *is better* than the others" debate. The service management community seems to have polarized to a specific framework and developed a bit of "tunnel vision." Currently, ITIL is the "most widely accepted approach to IT service management in the world."[4] As robust as ITIL is, there are areas where the information provided is either lacking or incomplete (e.g. governance, risk, implementing a working service management system, etc.). Of course, this shouldn't create a negative impression but it is an opportunity for the Service Manager to explore the other frameworks.

So, let's level set. First, all service management frameworks support the goal of delivering quality services that benefit the business efficiently, effectively and economically. This is not an unknown to anyone in the service management field. It's why they (and their organization) have adopted and adapted the

---

[3] We recognize the many service management frameworks, standards, methodologies as well as the particular nature of those terms. For ease of reading, we will use the term "framework" to represent all unless we are specifically speaking to an international standard.

[4] *www.axelos.com/best-practice-solutions/itil*

framework of their choice. However, the quandary is this: no matter what framework has been chosen, there are gaps. These gaps become more and more noticeable as one explores all available frameworks.

Second, if we agree there are gaps, we also must agree the various frameworks all have specific strengths – there is a reason why there are so many frameworks – they were developed because what was available had gaps! This is just simple logic. Service managers then need to recognize the gaps and then exploit the strengths found in the service management frameworks. As in life, there is no time or place for bigotry!

Third, most service managers have taken one or more certification classes. Well done. As good as most training is, it is not a substitute for experience. The academic deployment of framework guidance is typically doomed from the start; often creating greater disruption than the original situation which was supposed to improve with the deployment of best practice. Knowledge does not equate success.

We also recognize there will be controversy around what we have written. That is the beauty of applying frameworks – there never is an absolute. As long as one can justify, document and demonstrate the benefit sought has been achieved, there is no "wrong." Can the system improve? Absolutely and always – we are firm believers in continual improvement knowing the only constant in life is change. Thus, we encourage you to look for and communicate those improvements.

The Focus

This book focuses on four of the many available frameworks – we'd love to include "all" of them but we do have to define a scope or we would never be done. Therefore, we chose (in no particular order) COBIT, ISO/IEC 20000-1, ITIL and CMMI-SVC. We felt these four would adequately support the intent of this book and offer a solid foundation on which to build. We will offer other frameworks for consideration where appropriate and encourage you to explore them to continually improve your service management initiative.

We chose these four for the following reasons:

- Availability of information
- Pervasiveness of deployment
- International acceptance
- A business need to create value
- Process orientation.

Please don't interpret the inclusion or omission of any of the many service management frameworks as a value-based decision. Each framework has a purpose and benefit. The four we've chosen creates a manageable level of information for this book which is to show how to deploy an amalgamated solution using the strengths of each. We will use caselets (mini case studies) to provide context – each caselet is fictitious but based on real events from our consulting careers. We've chosen some rather generic and common events to demonstrate how to combine the best practices.

Strengths

While each of the frameworks is described in the next chapter, we thought it appropriate to list the strengths as we see them for these four frameworks.

- COBIT
  - o Ability to conduct process capability assessment
  - o Metrics
  - o RACI diagrams to show interrelationships
- ISO/IEC 20000-1
  - o Concise listing of what MUST be achieved
  - o Service Management System (SMS)
- ITIL
  - o Well-described processes
  - o Generic information around lifecycle activities.
- CMMI-SVC
  - o Organizational supports for improvement
  - o Defines an evolutionary path for improvement

Combining these strengths, you can readily see the following benefits:

- An overall management system for the service management activities (SMS)
  - o Business-based philosophy based on Deming's PCDA
- Processes to support the lifecycle service delivery
  - o Interrelationships of processes for efficiency
- Descriptions of the various maturity levels within the processes (drives improvements)
  - o Measuring process performance
- Organizational support of the portfolio of services from the enterprise perspective
  - o Integrated management of multiple services

The Five Anchors and Caselets

Chapter 4 will hold the main content – an analysis structure, which we call the Five Anchors, developed to ensure an enterprise-wide assessment. The Five Anchors are applied to five caselets to show how to not only analyse the situations but also apply multiple frameworks towards a common goal.

When used, this analysis structure, based on practical experience as well as guidance from the service management frameworks, is a consistent view into any scenario. We've then applied various frameworks to provide information and best practices that an organization can adopt/adapt creating a solution to benefit the business.

To assist in your learning, a comprehensive mapping between COBIT, ISO/IEC 20000-1, ITIL and CMMI-SVC, can be found in Appendix A. We recognize the 37 processes described in COBIT do not necessarily create a one-to-one relationship with the processes in ISO/IEC 20000-1, ITIL and CMMI-SVC. We used each framework's numbering scheme to point to specific references rather than regurgitate the information held within these frameworks. For full comprehension and to compare the information, you will need to view the full references.

CHAPTER 2: COBIT, ISO/IEC 20000, ITIL AND CMMI-SVC

While most will recognize and have in-depth knowledge of one or two of these service management philosophies, we thought it necessary to level-set not only the core structural information, but to also describe the improvement models that are integral to each framework.

Overview of COBIT

COBIT is a business framework for the governance and management of enterprise IT. With aspects in security, quality and compliance, its focus is not necessarily on how to execute a process, but rather what should be done to ensure proper control of that process. Therefore, you won't technically implement COBIT from the bottom up, but use it as a tool to help you control processes from the top down as a part of a larger governance initiative.

Starting out as a tool designed for IT auditors to assist in the control of IT, it has grown into a model to assist with compliance requirements as well. It helps enterprises understand IT systems and guides decisions around the level of security, risk and control that is necessary to protect assets through the leverage of an IT governance model.

By using stakeholder needs as the starting point for governance and management activities, COBIT offers a holistic and integrated view of enterprise governance and management of IT that uses consistent and common language. This framework has many rich capabilities, notably the introduction of GEIT (Governance of Enterprise IT) principles, increased focus on enablers, new and modified processes, the separation of governance and management, revised and expanded goals and metrics and a new process capability model to name just a few.

There are several documents and tools to choose from in the overall COBIT product family. These can be found at *www.isaca.org/cobit* and include:

- *COBIT 5, A Business Framework for the Governance and Management of Enterprise IT*[5]
- COBIT 5 Enabler Guides
    - o *COBIT 5 Enabling Processes*
    - o *COBIT 5 Enabling Information*
    - o Other Enabler Guides to be developed
- COBIT 5 Professional Guides
    - o *COBIT 5 Implementation*
    - o *COBIT 5 for Information Security*
    - o *COBIT 5 for Assurance*
    - o *COBIT 5 for Risk*
    - o Other professional guides to be developed.

The building blocks of the COBIT framework are leveraged through the use of five principles and seven enablers (see Figure 1).

- Principles
    - o Meeting Stakeholder Needs
    - o Covering the Enterprise End-to-End
    - o Applying a Single Integrated Framework
    - o Enabling a Holistic Approach
    - o Separating Governance from Management.

Note that the Principle "Enabling a Holistic Approach" gives rise to the Enablers.

- Enablers (see Figure 2)
    - o Principles, Policies and Frameworks
    - o Processes
    - o Organizational Structures
    - o Culture, Ethics and Behaviour
    - o Information
    - o Services, Infrastructure and Applications
    - o People, Skills and Competencies.

---

[5] Free to members and non-members of ISACA. All other volumes are available for purchase for non-members.

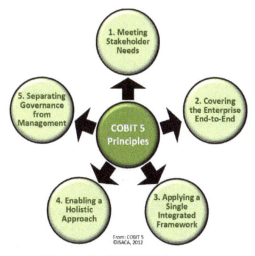

Figure 1: COBIT Principles

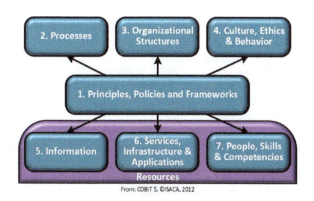

Figure 2: COBIT Enablers

At the core of any framework are processes. COBIT has 37 processes in five domains.

- **Evaluate, Direct, Monitor (EDM)** – includes processes that address stakeholder governance objectives, specifically benefits delivery and risk and resource optimization. Additional process activities stress the evaluation of strategic options, hence providing direction to IT. The processes supporting the EDM domain include:
  o EDM 1: Ensure Governance Framework Setting and Maintenance
  o EDM 2: Ensure Benefits Delivery
  o EDM 3: Ensure Risk Optimization
  o EDM 4: Ensure Resource Optimization
  o EDM 5: Ensure Stakeholder Transparency.

- **Align, Plan & Organize (APO)** – directs solution delivery (BAI) as well as service delivery and support (DSS). Specific activities focus on strategy and tactics and how IT can impact the achievement of business objectives. These processes define the management system for IT and include:
  o APO 1: Manage the IT Framework
  o APO 2: Manage Strategy
  o APO 3: Manage Enterprise Architecture
  o APO 4: Manage Innovation
  o APO 5: Manage Portfolio
  o APO 6: Manage Budget and Costs
  o APO 7: Manage Human Resources
  o APO 8: Manage Relationships
  o APO 9: Manage Service Agreements
  o APO 10: Manage Suppliers
  o APO 11: Manage Quality
  o APO 12: Manage Risk
  o APO 13: Manage Security.

- **Build, Acquire & Implement (BAI)** – this domain provides the solutions based on the previously defined strategies and ensures the solution will support and enhance the business process. Change is also managed in this domain – again keeping the solution aligned with business objectives. The following 10 processes support the BAI objectives:

- o BAI 1: Manage Programs and Projects
- o BAI 2: Manage Requirements Definition
- o BAI 3: Manage Solutions Identification and Build
- o BAI 4: Manage Availability and Capacity
- o BAI 5: Manage Organizational Change Enablement
- o BAI 6: Manage Changes
- o BAI 7: Manage Change Acceptance and Transitioning
- o BAI 8: Manage Knowledge
- o BAI 9: Manage Assets
- o BAI 10: Manage Configuration.

- **Deliver, Service & Support (DSS)** – receives the solutions and deploys the necessary functionality for the user community. The focus of DSS is on the delivery and support services including security, continuity, support services and management of data and the environment. The processes include:
  - o DSS 1: Manage Operations
  - o DSS 2: Manage Service Requests and Incidents
  - o DSS 3: Manage Problems
  - o DSS 4: Manage Continuity
  - o DSS 5: Manage Security Services
  - o DSS 6: Manage Business Process Controls.

- **Monitor, Evaluate & Assess (MEA)** – monitors processes to ensure compliance as well as achievement of the necessary assurance levels. Key areas within this domain include performance management, regulatory compliance, governance and internal control monitoring. Processes supporting these activities include:
  - o MEA 1: Monitor, Evaluate and Assess Performance and Conformance
  - o MEA 2: Monitor, Evaluate and Assess the System of Internal Control
  - o MEA 3: Monitor, Evaluate and Assess Compliance with External Requirements.

These five domains support the separation of governance and management by aligning EDM with governance processes and BAI, DSS and MEA with a typical Plan-Build-Run-Monitor approach. See Figure 3.

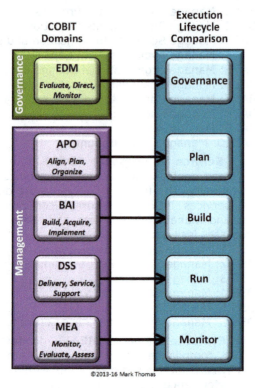

Figure 3: COBIT Domains to Lifecycle Activities

COBIT

Governance of Enterprise IT | *Management of Enterprise IT*

EVALUATE, DIRECT & MONITOR (EDM)	ALIGN, PLAN & ORGANIZE (APO)	BUILD, ACQUIRE & IMPLEMENT (BAI)	DELIVER, SERVICE & SUPPORT (DSS)	MONITOR, EVALUATE & ASSESS (MEA)
EDM1 Ensure Governance Framework Setting and Maintenance	APO1 Manage the IT Framework	BAI1 Manage Programs and Projects	DSS1 Manage Operations	MEA1 Monitor, Evaluate, and Assess Performance and Conformance
EDM2 Benefits Delivery	APO2 Manage Strategy	BAI2 Manage Requirements Definition	DSS2 Manage Service Requests & Incidents	MEA2 Monitor, Evaluate and Assess the System of Internal Control
EDM3 Ensure Risk Optimization	APO3 Manage Enterprise Architecture	BAI3 Manage Solutions Identification and Build	DSS3 Manage Problems	MEA3 Monitor, Evaluate and Assess Compliance with External Requirements
EDM4 Ensure Resource Optimization	APO4 Manage Innovation	BAI4 Manage Availability and Capacity	DSS4 Manage Continuity	
EDM5 Ensure Stakeholder Transparency	APO5 Manage Portfolio	BAI5 Manage Organizational Change Enablement	DSS5 Manage Security Services	
	APO6 Manage Budget & Costs	BAI6 Manage Changes	DSS6 Manage Business Process Controls	
	APO7 Manage Human Resources	BAI7 Manage Change Acceptance and Transitioning		
	APO8 Manage Relationships	BAI8 Manage Knowledge		
	APO9 Manage Service Agreements	BAI9 Manage Assets		
	APO10 Manage Suppliers	BAI10 Manage Configuration		
	APO11 Manage Quality			
	APO12 Manage Risk			
	APO13 Manage Security			

Table 1: COBIT Domains and Processes

ISO/IEC 20000-1:2011

Author's Note: The ISO/IEC 20000 family of standards is currently under revision. There are several mandatory changes that will impact Parts 1-5 over the next 18 months. Part 1 will be standardized to the current model for management system standards, thus allowing comparison and congruence. With these changes to Part 1, the remaining parts will be updated to remain aligned to the structure and new requirements. When the new version of the Standard becomes publicly available, a new mapping table will also be released.

The ISO/IEC 20000 family of documents define the international standard for IT Service Management with a goal of establishing a common reference for IT service delivery. There are several parts to the Standard, which revolve around the auditable Part 1 (26 pages) and includes:

- Part 1: Service management system requirements
- Part 2: Guidance on the application of service management systems
- Part 3: Guidance on scope definition and applicability of ISO/IEC 20000-1
- Part 4: Process reference model [Technical Report][6]
- Part 5: Exemplar implementation plan for ISO/IEC 20000-1 [Technical Report]
- Part 6: Requirements for bodies providing audit and certification of service management systems[3]
- Part 9: Guidance on the application of ISO/IEC 20000-1 to cloud services [Technical Report]
- Part 10: Concepts and terminology [Technical Report]
- Part 11: Guidance on the relationship between ISO/IEC 20000-1:2011 and related service management frameworks: ITIL® [Technical Report]
- Part 12: Guidance on the relationship between ISO/IEC 20000-1:2011 and related service management frameworks: CMMI-SVC® [Technical Report].

Simply, Part 1 defines the internationally accepted requirements for the Service Management System (SMS) which include the "...design, transition, delivery and improvement of services that

---

[6] Under review – currently in preliminary status

fulfil service requirements and provide value for both the customer and service provider."[7]

Developed originally as a UK national Standard (BS 15000), the early "edition" was a method allowing consistent measurement indicating compliance to ITIL 'best practices,' thus allowing organizations to declare themselves compliant. The international community quickly saw the benefit of BS 15000 and moved it through the process to create the international Standard, ISO/IEC 20000-1:2005. ISO/IEC 20000 continually improves following and driving ITIL improvements. Incorrectly known as the "ITIL Standard," ISO/IEC 20000 is a service management product in its own right. It demands an integrated process approach based in the PDCA methodology across all aspects of the SMS and services. Combining the SMS with the PDCA drives value-driven service delivery, customer satisfaction and monitored, reviewed and improved services based on objectives and agreed measurements.

The unique aspect of ISO/IEC 20000-1 is the definition of a service management system. A service provider must "...plan, establish, implement, operate, monitor, review, maintain and improve an SMS" throughout the span of service activities (e.g. design, transition, delivery and improvement). Specifically, the SMS includes very clear requirements for management responsibility, governance of processes operated by other parties, document and resource management and the explicit activities of establishing and improving the SMS following the PDCA methodologies.

The SMS provides the management foundation for the well-known service management processes divided into four main groupings:

- **Service Delivery** (Service Level Management, Service Reporting, Service Continuity and Availability Management, Budgeting/Accounting, Capacity Management, Information Security Management)
- **Relationship** (Business Relationship Management, Supplier Management)

---

[7] ISO/IEC 20000-1:2011, Information Technology – Service Management – Part 1: Service management system requirements

- **Resolution** (Incident and Service Request Management, Problem Management)
- **Control** (Configuration Management, Change Management, Release and Deployment Management).

Lastly, there is an overall set of requirements for the design and transition of new or changed services. This set of requirements nicely defines the flow of activities beginning with planning for the new or changed service (e.g. requirements gathering, resource management, communication, testing, dependencies, service acceptance criteria, etc.) and progressing through the design, development and transitioning of the new or changed service. Retiring an obsolete service falls under this section as well.

Part 1 is brilliant in its brevity – the requirements are concise and clear. What is not provided by Part 1 is the "how to do." Part 2 and the other Parts provide further clarification and great insight to the requirements as well as specific examples to fulfil the requirements but, again, the "how to do" is still not prescribed. It is clearly up to the organization and their unique working environment to define how to meet the requirements and then document them. ISO/IEC 20000 family of documents is, in our opinion, the place to start any information gathering for an "adopt and adapt" initiative. Then utilize the other Service Management frameworks and standards as a body of knowledge to complete the "how."

Table 2 lists the processes and the corresponding section numbering from the source document. These numbers are important to the mapping information found the Appendix.

ISO/IEC 20000-1: 2011 Processes

4 Service Management System Requirements	5 Design and transition of new or changed services	6 Service Delivery Processes	7 Relationship Processes	8 Resolution Processes	9 Control Processes
4.1 Management Responsibility	5.1 General	6.1 Service level management	7.1 Business relationship management	8.1 Incident Management	9.1 Configuration Management
4.2 Governance of processes operated by other parties	5.2 Plan new or changed services	6.2 Service reporting	7.2 Supplier management	8.2 Problem Management	9.2 Change Management
4.3 Documentation Management	5.3 Design and development of new or changed services	6.3 Service continuity and availability management			9.3 Release and deployment management
4.4 Resource Management	5.4 Transition of new or changed services	6.4 Budgeting and accounting for services			
4.5 Establish and improve the SMS		6.5 Capacity management			
4.5.1 Define Scope		6.6 Information security management			
4.5.2 Plan the SMS (Plan)					
4.5.3 Implement and operate the SMS (Do)					
4.5.4 Monitor and review the SMS (Check)					
5.4.4 Maintain and improve the SMS (Act)					

Table 2: ISO/IEC 20000-1 Processes

Overview of ITIL

The Information Technology Infrastructure Library (ITIL) describes a framework of best practices for the provision of quality services. ITIL is only one of part of a suite of publications that describe IT service management. The activities, processes, functions and capabilities documented in ITIL provide guidance that should be analysed by an organization to define an 'adopt and adapt' program of activities to improve service delivery based on their individual needs, culture, organizational structure and so on. The use of public frameworks and standards benefit the organization as the "wheel isn't reinvented" and the organization can create their own efficiencies from what has already been learned.

ITIL® Service Lifecycle Publications, 2011 Edition

Figure 4: The ITIL Lifecycle

So where do these 'best practices' originate? ITIL is based on various sources (e.g. standards, industry practices, academic research, training and education and internal experience) though the work of a variety practitioners (e.g. employees, customers, suppliers, advisers and technologies). Business requirements (e.g. legal, regulatory, customers, corporate mission, etc.) create knowledge that is fit for business purposes and has defined objectives, a specific context and measurable purpose.

As a 'public domain' set of best practices, the information held within ITIL is more likely to be used and improved via use and as such, offers an advantage over proprietary knowledge and processes. Thus, a great deal of the success of ITIL has been because the information has been readily and easily available and the vocabulary used in the books has found general acceptance. Additionally, ITIL is vendor-neutral, non-prescriptive and represents best practices from industry leaders of best-in-class service providers. Adopting ITIL enables organizations to:

- Deliver value to customers through services
- Integrate service strategy with business strategy and customer need
- Measure, monitor and optimize IT services
- Manage risk
- Manage knowledge
- Manage capabilities and resources
- Adopt a standard approach to Service Management
- Change organizational culture to support achievement of sustained success
- Improve interaction and relationships with customers
- Optimize and reduce cost.

ITIL is based on the concept of a five-stage service lifecycle. A brief description of each stage is below:

- **Service Strategy (SS)** – strategy is the source of value creation as it is grounded in the understanding of organizational objectives and customer needs. Concepts such as provider types, market spaces, service assets and the service portfolio are critical to this lifecycle stage. Processes supporting SS include:
  - o Strategy Management for IT Services (StM)
  - o Service Portfolio Management (SPM)
  - o Financial Management for IT Services (FM)
  - o Demand Management (DM)
  - o Business Relationship Management (BRM)
- **Service Design (SD)** – the stage that turns the service strategy into plans that will deliver business objectives. Key

concepts of design and development, management systems, technology and architecture, process design and designing measurement systems are central to the activities within SD. Processes supporting these activities include:

  o Design Coordination (DC)
  o Service Catalogue Management (SCatM)
  o Service Level Management (SLM)
  o Availability Management (AM)
  o Capacity Management (CapM)
  o IT Service Continuity Management (ITSCM)
  o Information Security Management (ISM)
  o Supplier Management (SuppM)

- **Service Transition (ST)** – focuses on the processes necessary to deliver new or changed services (or removing a service) with the fundamental purpose of controlling risk. ST ensures the value identified in SS is effectively transitioned to operation. Processes that support the ST activities include:

  o Transition Planning and Support (TPS)
  o Change Management (ChM)
  o Service Asset and Configuration Management (SACM)
  o Release and Deployment Management (RDM)
  o Service Validation and Testing (SVT)
  o Change Evaluation (ChE)
  o Knowledge Management (KM)

- **Service Operation (SO)** – includes the "visible" activities of the service provider – the agreed, designed and transitioned services are now available (visible). The activities and processes of SO all focus on the concept of value delivery not only to the customer and user, but also the service provider. Both proactive and reactive activities dominate this stage, again with the purpose of meeting the current and future needs of the business and service provider alike. Processes and functions (in italics) that support the SO activities include:

  o Event Management (EM)
  o Incident Management (IM)
  o Request Fulfilment (RF)
  o Problem Management (PM)
  o Access Management (AccM)
  o *Service Desk*

- o *Technical Management (TM)*
- o *IT Operations Management (ITOpsM)*
- o *Application Management (AppM)*
- **Continual Service Improvement (CSI)** – focuses on the activities that support improvement initiatives within strategy, design, transition and operational activities. Using principles and practices from quality management, CSI links improvement activities to the ongoing needs of the business. Grounded in Deming's Plan-Do-Check-Act (PDCA) methodology, CSI concentrates on elements of service measurement, reporting and assessments.
  - o 7-Step Improvement Process (7S)

More information around ITIL and its educational schema can be found at *www.axelos.com/best-practice-solutions/itil*.

Table 3 lists the processes and the corresponding section numbering from the source documents. These numbers are important to the mapping information found the Appendix.

ITIL Processes and Functions

SS Service Strategy	SD Service Design	ST Service Transition	SO Service Operation	CSI Continual Service Improvement
4.1 Strategy Management for IT Services (StM)	4.1 Design Coordination (DC)	4.1 Transition Planning & Support (TPS)	4.1 Event Management (EM)	4.1 Seven Step Improvement (7S)
4.2 Service Portfolio Management (SPM)	4.2 Service Catalog Management (SCatM)	4.2 Change Management (ChM)	4.2 Incident Management (IM)	
4.3 Financial Management for IT Services (FM)	4.3 Service Level Management (SLM)	4.3 Service Asset and Configuration Management (SACM)	4.3 Request Fulfillment (RF)	
4.4 Demand Management (DM)	4.4 Availability Management (AM)	4.4 Release and Deployment Management (RDM)	4.4 Problem Management (PM)	
4.5 Business Relationship Management (BRM)	4.5 Capacity Management (CapM)	4.5 Service Validation & Testing (SVT)	4.5 Access Management (AccM)	
	4.6 IT Service Continuity Management (ITSCM)	4.6 Change Evaluation (ChE)		
	4.7 Information Security Management (ISM)	4.7 Knowledge Management (KM)		
	4.8 Supplier Management (SuppM)			

Functions
6.3 Service Desk
6.4 Technical Management
6.5 IT Operations Management
6.6 Application Management

Table 3: ITIL Lifecycle Processes and Functions

Overview of CMMI-SVC

The CMMI®, or Capability Maturity Model Integration, is an improvement approach that organizes a set of effective practices to improve business performance (for example, cost, schedule, customer satisfaction, productivity, quality). There are currently three focus areas, or *models*, within the CMMI:

- CMMI for Development (CMMI-DEV) V1.3 – for product and service development.
- CMMI for Acquisition (CMMI-ACQ) V1.3 – for product and service acquisition.
- CMMI for Services (CMMI-SVC) V1.3 – for service establishment and management.

CMMI-SVC guides all types of service providers to establish, manage and improve services to meet business goals. CMMI-SVC can be applied internally or externally and is easily integrated with other improvement or quality frameworks, such as ITIL or ISO/IEC 20000-1. Similar to the previous frameworks discussed, CMMI-SVC describes 'what' to do, not 'how' to do it. It is a true framework, with a twist. The practices in CMMI-SVC provide a consistent benchmark as a basis for process improvement. So, organizations that have adopted and adapted CMMI-SVC practices can choose to undergo an *appraisal* to receive a maturity rating (unlike ISO/IEC 20000-1, there is no certification in CMMI-SVC), which allows the organization to plan for continual improvement, based on business need.

The fundamental building block of a CMMI model is a process area (PA). There are 24 PAs in CMMI-SVC where 16 PAs are core, meaning they are common to the other models (CMMI-DEV, CMMI-ACQ). These core PAs support the basic activities across services, development and acquisition. Of the remaining eight PAs, seven are unique to CMMI-SVC and the eighth is shared between CMMI-SVC and CMMI-DEV (see Figure 5).

The CMMI-SVC Service PAs include:

- **Capacity and Availability Management (CAM)** – ensuring there are appropriate amounts of resource to deliver services and they are available when needed at an appropriate cost.

- **Incident Resolution and Prevention** (**IRP**) – handling what goes wrong and preventing it from going wrong if possible.
- **Service Continuity** (**SCON**) – being ready to recover from a disaster and continue to deliver services as agreed.
- **Service Delivery** (**SD**) – the focus is on service agreements, defining the service delivery approach, managing service requests and operating the service system.
- **Service System Development** (**SSD**) – ensuring all necessary people, processes, consumables and equipment to deliver the service is available.
- **Service System Transition** (**SST**) – deploying new systems, changing existing systems, or retiring obsolete systems while managing risk.
- **Strategic Service Management** (**STSM**) – defining the services that will be provided, standardizing the offering and communicating the availability of those services.

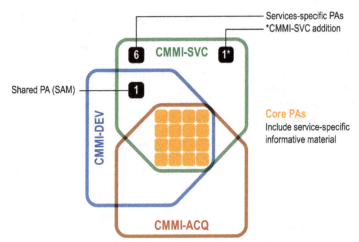

This Figure is from CMMI® Institute "Introduction to CMMI for Services Training" © 2016 CMMI® Institute

Figure 5: CMMI-SVC

The 24 PAs can be grouped in the following categories:

- **Define, Establish and Deliver Services**
  o Service Delivery (SD)
  o Requirements Management (REQM)
  o Work Planning (WP)
  o Service System Development (SSD)
- **Monitor and Control Service and Work Products**
  o Capacity and Availability Management (CAM)
  o Work Monitoring and Control (WMC)
  o Configuration Management (CM)
- **Ensure Service Mission Success**
  o Incident Resolution and Prevention (IRP)
  o Risk Management (RSKM)
  o Service Continuity (SCON)
  o Service System Transition (SST)
- **Make Work Explicit and Measurable**
  o Measurement and Analysis (MA)
  o Organizational Process Performance (OPP)
  o Quantitative Work Management (QWM)
  o Causal Analysis and Resolution (CAR)
  o Organizational Performance Management (OPM)
- **Manage Decisions, Suppliers and Standard Services**
  o Supplier Agreement Management (SAM)
  o Decision Analysis and Resolution (DAR)
  o Strategic Service Management (STSM)
- **Create a Culture to Sustain Service Excellence**
  o Process and Product Quality Assurance (PPQA)
  o Organizational Process Definition (OPD)
  o Integrated Work Management (IWM)
  o Organizational Training (OT)
  o Organizational Process Focus (OPF)

The structure of each of these PAs is as follows:

- One or more Specific Goals (SG) with a corresponding set of one or more Specific Practices (SP)
  o SPs describe the activities necessary to achieve the SG.
- Application of Generic Goals (GG) with supporting Generic Practices (GP)
  o Generic practices apply to all process areas – they are reminders to follow the process and are the expected

model components. They represent the institutionalization of the model components.

Fully detailing the Specific Goals and Practices of each of the 24 PAs is beyond the scope of this book and associated mapping. This information is readily available in the full documentation as well as a full mapping between CMMI-SVC and ISO/IEC 20000 in ISO/IEC 20000-12 (*www.iso.org*).

There are three GGs with a number of associated GPs that collectively represent the activities necessary for process *institutionalization* (an activity ingrained in the culture and behaviour of an organization). The generic goals advance the maturity (for example, performed, managed, defined) of an organization's processes as each GG and corresponding GPs are met. The GGs and associated GPs are:

- **GG 1**   **Achieve Specific Goals**
  - o   GP 1.1   Perform Specific Practices
- **GG 2**   **Institutionalize a Managed Process**
  - o   GP 2.1   Establish an Organizational Policy
  - o   GP 2.2   Plan the Process
  - o   GP 2.3   Provide Resources
  - o   GP 2.4   Assign Responsibility
  - o   GP 2.5   Train People
  - o   GP 2.6   Control Work Products
  - o   GP 2.7   Identify and Involve Relevant Stakeholders
  - o   GP 2.8   Monitor and Control the Process
  - o   GP 2.9   Objectively Evaluate Adherence
  - o   GP 2.10   Review Status with Higher Level Management
- **GG 3**   **Institutionalize a Defined Process**
  - o   GP 3.1   Establish a Defined Process
  - o   GP 3.2   Collect Process Related Experiences

CMMI-SVC   v1.3   can   be   downloaded   here: *http://cmmiinstitute.com/resources/cmmi-services-version-13*.

Table 4 lists the processes and the corresponding section numbering from the source documents. These numbers are important to the mapping information found in the Appendix.

CMMI-SVC

Process Areas (PAs)
Specific Goals (SGs) and Specific Practices (SPs) are not listed

DEFINE, ESTABLISH & DELIVER SERVICES	MONITOR & CONTROL SERVICES & WORK PRODUCTS	ENSURE SERVICE MISSION SUCCESS	MAKE WORK EXPLICIT & MEASURABLE	MANAGE DECISIONS, SUPPLIERS & STANDARD SERVICES	CREATE A CULTURE TO SUSTAIN SERVICE EXCELLENCE	GENERIC GOALS* (GGs)
SD Service Delivery	CAM Capacity & Availability Management	IRP Incident Resolution & Prevention	MA Measurement & Analysis	SAM Supplier Agreement Management	PPQA Process & Product Quality Assurance	GG 1 Achieve Specific Goals
REQM Requirements Management	WMC Work Monitoring & Control	RSKM Risk Management	OPP Organizational Process Performance	DAR Decision Analysis & Resolution	OPD Organizational Process Definition	GG 2 Institutionalize a Managed Process
WP Work Planning	CM Configuration Management	SCON Service Continuity	QWM Quantitative Work Management	STSM Strategic Service Management	IWM Integrated Work Management	GG 3 Institutionalize a Defined Process
SSD Service System Development		SST Service System Transition	CAR Causal Analysis & Resolution		OT Organizational Training	*Generic Practices (GPs) are not listed
			OPM Organizational Performance Management		OPF Organizational Process Focus	*Applicable as stand-alone goals or to specific PAs

Table 4: Table 4: Interrelated Components and their Associated Steps

Improvement Models

IT Governance Implementation Model

Within *COBIT 5 Implementation*, the "Implementation Life Cycle" is the core concept and is key to the COBIT framework. This reference guide provides a good practice approach to continual improvement that can be used to implement the various components of a governance framework. As with all improvement lifecycles, it can be tailored to meet specific enterprise needs.

It is well-known that any improvement initiative should be driven by the business need of creating value and to ensure that this value is realized, adoption of efforts should be viewed from several different perspectives. Additionally, efforts should have the right mix of sponsorship, proper scope, well-understood objectives and should fit the overall appetite for change that the enterprise can absorb.

The implementation lifecycle, illustrated in Figure 6, provides a methodology for organizations to leverage clearly defined (iterative) steps to adopt the COBIT framework. The three interrelated components and their associated steps are shown in Table 5.

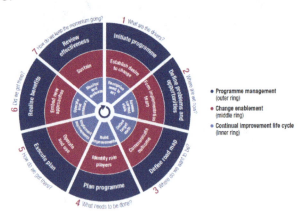

Figure 6: The Implementation Lifecycle
***COBIT 5 Implementation Guide*, ISACA**

COBIT Implementation Model
Interrelated Components and their Associated Steps

	Phase 1	Phase 2	Phase 3	Phase 4	Phase 5	Phase 6	Phase 7
	What are the drivers?	Where are we now?	Where do we want to be?	What needs to be done?	How do we get there?	Did we get there?	How do we keep the momentum going?
Program Management (PM)	Initiate program	Define problems and opportunities	Define roadmap	Plan program	Execute plan	Realize benefits	Review effectiveness
Change Enablement (CE)	Establish desire to change	Form implementation team	Communicate outcome	Identify role players	Operate and use	Embed new approaches	Sustain
Continual Improvement Lifecycle (CI)	Recognize need to act	Assess current state	Define target state	Build improvements	Implement improvements	Operate and measure	Monitor and evaluate

Table 5: Interrelated Components and their Associated Steps

This approach clearly indicates that all three components need to be addressed and that they are interrelated – any major improvement effort (like the deployment of a new or changed service or process) requires the control that good program management will bring as well as some changes within the organization, specifically, understand and addressing the organizational change tolerance as well as developing and enhancing the cultural environment for continual improvement. There are seven phases; each defining a main activity within that component. The seven phases are:

- **Phase 1: What are the drivers?** Identifies the need for improvement by capturing and addressing change drivers and trigger events (pain points) and subsequently, creates a desire to change from an executive level, documented in a business case.
- **Phase 2: Where are we now?** The focus of this phase is defining current capability by defining enterprise and IT-related goals via the Goals Cascade. These elements will guide a process capability assessment, with the end result answering "where we are now" based on the pre-defined desired state.
- **Phase 3: Where do we want to be?** Improvement targets are set based on the process capability assessment. These results will define the gap between the as-is and the to-be state which identify improvement opportunities.
- **Phase 4: What needs to be done?** Improvement solutions are documented noting that some may be very quick wins and others may have much longer implementation timelines. Define the projects based on priority of the projects overall contribution to overall business objectives.
- **Phase 5: How do we get there?** Deploy the practical solution meeting the various objectives defined in the previous steps. Ensure good measures are defined, deployed and monitored to ensure continued alignment with business objectives as well as continued engagement of top management and other stakeholders.
- **Phase 6: Did we get there?** Continue monitoring and ensure no recidivism in order to achieve the expected benefits.
- **Phase 7: How do we keep the momentum going?** Review the program success, any new governance or

management requirements and reinforce the need for continual improvement.

PDCA

Many process-based management systems (i.e. ISO9001, ISO/IEC 20000, ISO/IEC 27001, etc.) are underpinned by the Deming Cycle (Plan-Do-Check-Act - PDCA). The power of this methodology is in its absolute simplicity – four easy to understand steps that drive continual review and assessment of a process or activity. Briefly, PDCA can be condensed as such:

- **Plan** – objectives, policies, plans are defined for a process, service, system.
- **Do** – implement the process, service, system.
- **Check** – monitor and measure the activities and outcomes against the objectives, policies and requirements; report on the results.
- **Act** – based on the assessed results, take actions to improve the performance.

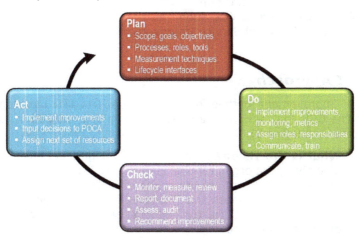

Figure 7: Deming's PDCA

PDCA is meant to be iterative with each cycle moving the process closer and closer to the defined "ultimate" goal. What is interesting is that the success of PDCA is based on the capture of knowledge from previous iterations. This increase of knowledge within each iteration allows one to refine the ultimate goal, which may very well be an initial "best guess," to something that is more appropriate and focused on true business need. This methodology allows for movement where the sometimes overwhelming "ready, aim, aim, aim, aim, aim…." actions of getting it "perfect" the first time and never accomplishing anything are now replaced with a "ready, aim, fire, aim, fire" action. Between each "aim, fire" sequence, the lessons learned are applied to the next. This is more "forgiving" than having a specific, "set in stone" goal that on paper, is fantastic but when operationalized, very unrealistic. Now, learning and improvement are a constant rather than a side-effect of, possibly, a very expensive and limited value exercise.

PDCA underpins the activities and processes of the Service Management System (SMS) as described in ISO/IEC 20000-1. Also, it is quite easy to see where the ITIL Service Lifecycle holds the PDCA elements:

- **Plan** – Service Strategy and Service Design
- **Do** – Service Transition
- **Check** – Service Operation
- **Act** – Continual Service Improvement.

CSI Approach

One improvement method found within the 2011 ITIL literature is the CSI Approach. This approach can be summarized in six steps (see figure 8):

- **What is the vision?** – understand the high-level business objectives, the organizational culture and environment (is it ready to or can it embrace the changes?), ensure the alignment of business and IT strategies, specifically linking the improvement to the benefit and support of the organizational directions.
- **Where are you now?** – complete a baseline maturity assessment against a known standard or benchmark (ISO/IEC 20000-1, COBIT, SWOT analysis, etc.) where people (skills and competencies; values and beliefs), process, products (technology and tools) and partners (suppliers and partners) are fully analysed.

- **Where do you want to be?** – agree and prioritize the improvements that represent the steps necessary to achieve the vision thus setting specific goals and objectives (SMART) across the enterprise within a manageable timeframe.
- **How do we get there?** – implement a detailed plan based on the improvements previously defined to improve service and process quality.
- **Did we get there?** – define a series of measurements and metrics to measure progress to the agreed milestones, but also ensure compliance to the new process or service activities.
- **How do we keep the momentum going?** – using measures and metrics, organizational change techniques and good management to ensure changes become embedded in the organization and there is no opportunity or tolerance for recidivism and then start the cycle again – review vision and objectives, identify new improvements, etc.

Deming's PDCA can easily be seen in this model with the first three steps fulfilling "Plan" and then the remaining steps match up directly with the final three Deming components.

This approach is valid in any and every aspect of the business. Frankly, we have followed this model on our consulting engagements – it's clear and simple and it demands a focus on the business need, thus providing value for the customer and service provider. Apply this model not only to in-place services and functions but also to the ones that are only in the planning or 'pre-planning' stages. Following this specific model can prevent design flaws, provide focus for strategic activities and improve transition measures and on-going operational activities because the focus is on the end goal – achievement of business outcome. The question "how does the proposed improvement allow for the achievement of organizational goals?" is now definitively answered.

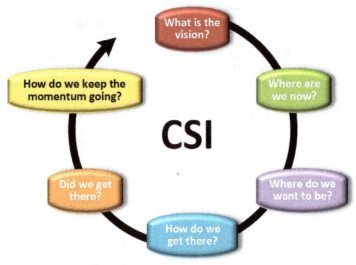

ITIL® Service Lifecycle Publications, 2011 Edition

Figure 8: CSI Approach

The IDEAL(SM) Model

The IDEAL Model has evolved from a lifecycle software process improvement model based on the Capability Maturity Model® (CMM®) to a more generically applicable continuous improvement approach. There are five phases, each with a set of activities, which defines a disciplined approach to improvement. Core to this model is the management of improvement as well as the development of an improvement strategy. The IDEAL Model clearly elaborates the PDCA cycle. The five phases and associated activities, shown as sub-bullets (see Figure 9), are:

- **I – Initiating**: defines the foundation for a successful improvement initiative; critical to the overall success of the improvement – if not done, subsequent phase activities consume resources with no clear benefit
  - Stimulus for change (business reason for change)
  - Set context (where does the improvement fit in the organization's business strategy?)

- o Build sponsorship (who is the champion of the initiative?)
- o Charter infrastructure (define the necessary resources along with expectations of performance and responsibilities)
- **D – Diagnosing**: defines 'where you are now' relative to 'where you want to be'
- o Characterize current and desired states (define the baseline as well as the desired end state)
- o Develop recommendations (use experts to map the way forward)
- **E – Establishing**: defines the work plan to achieve stated goal
- o Set priorities (define priorities of the improvement based on resources, dependencies, external factors and so on)
- o Develop approach (use information from the diagnosing phase with defined priorities)
- o Plan actions (develop the implementation plan)
- **A – Acting**: performing the defined plan
- o Create solution (generate a solution based on existing and new tools, processes, knowledge and skills)
- o Pilot/Test solution (once the solution is created, run a pilot)
- o Refine solution (based on results of pilot/test, refine the solution as needed; usually several iterations are required)
- o Implement solution (once workable, roll-out following the deployment plan)
- **L – Learning**: a 'lessons learned' phase to improve iterations of the model
- o Analyse and validate (review outcomes and the process that produced the outcome. Was the intended purpose met? Was the process to deploy the improvement efficient? Were business needs met?)
- o Propose future actions (based on the analysis, recommend improvements for the overall process to be confirmed by management)

This Figure is from Handbook: "IDEALSM: A User's Guide for Software Process Improvement" by Bob McFeeley, CMU/SEI 96-HB-001, © February 1996

Figure 9: The IDEAL Model

Summary

It is clear these four improvement models have a bit of overlap. The main point here is this: as a Service Manager, you adopt and adapt a model – be it the Implementation Lifecycle, Deming, the CSI Approach, or the IDEAL Model, or one of the many other models available. Or better yet, create something that works for you and your clients, always remembering the many elements to consider to ensure a robust improvement.

CHAPTER 3: ADDRESSING VSEs

Since publication of the first version, we've answered questions about how these frameworks can be applied to a small business. With that in mind, we've added this short section to relay this information to all.

There have been many developments within the Service Management community, specifically concerning the support of the very small enterprise (VSE). Too often the VSE is overlooked or ignored as a viable service provider or supplier to a service provider[8]. Research shows the VSE is often not capable of embracing and achieving international standard conformance if only due to the resources required (for example, time, effort, knowledge, costs and so on[9].

Although most standards state they are applicable to any size or type of organization; in reality, application requires 'expert' knowledge to size, adapt, or combine the requirements to fit the available resources and needs of the VSE. There is a 'learning curve' when adopting and adapting any framework no matter the size of the company, but maybe more so in the VSE.

Consider the 256 requirements of ISO/IEC 20000-1 (we only point out ISO/IEC 20000-1 because of the defined requirements to achieve certification). Depending on your perspective, 256 is either a really large or small number – to a VSE, it can be overwhelming. The IT shop might have only one or two staff, so how can they possibly fulfil all requirements? There are VSEs who have achieved the 20000 certificate but it wasn't without a great deal of creativity in combining and sizing the requirements to fit the needs of the organization while still fulfilling the requirements.

---

[8] OECD. *Organisation for Economic Co-operation and Development (OECD),* Small and Medium Enterprise *(SME) Outlook Report, 2005.*
[9] Land, S. K., Results of the IEEE Survey of Software Engineering Standards Users. Software Engineering Standards Symposium and Forum, 1997. Emerging International Standards. ISESS 97, Walnut Creek, CA, June 1–6, pp. 242 – 270, 1997.

So how can the VSE manage services and demonstrate conformance to a globally agreed set of requirements? ISO/IEC JTC1/SC7 (International Organization for Standardization (ISO) International Electrotechnical Commission (IEC) Joint Technical Committee 1 (JTC1) Sub-Committee 7 (SC7)) has a mandate to develop, maintain, promote and facilitate IT standards needed by global markets to meet business and user requirements concerning software and systems engineering. There are numerous working groups (WGs) supporting various aspects of software and systems engineering, but one in particular has a specific mandate to support the VSE – Working Group 24 (WG24).

WG24, System and Software Life Cycle Profiles and Guidelines for Very Small Enterprises (VSEs), was established to help the VSE by developing a set of profiles, many of them available at no cost, using subsets of requirements from appropriate standards. These profiles have been developed to improve product and/or service quality as well as process performance (see ISO/IEC 29110-1, Systems and software engineering -- Lifecycle profiles for Very Small Entities (VSEs) -- Part 1: Overview (*www.iso.org*). Additionally, each profile is auditable so the VSE gains the recognition they produce quality systems, system elements and /or services within their domain.

One such profile is being developed (at the time of press, these documents (ISO/IEC 29110-4-3 and ISO/IEC 29110-5-3) were under global review for formal publication) to address service delivery. Using requirements from ISO/IEC/IEEE 15288, ISO/IEC/IEEE 15289, ISO9000, ISO9001, ISO31000, ISO/IEC 38500 and ISO/IEC 10004, this profile defines processes for governance, operational control, relationship management, delivering warranty and the prevention or management of incidents. There are 19 requirements to achieve conformance to this profile. These 19 requirements are mapped to ISO/IEC 20000-1 so the VSE can pursue the certificate to demonstrate conformance to the requirements for a full Service Management System (SMS) when it is applicable to their business.

So, what does this mean for the VSE? The Five Anchors are applicable to any size organization and the mapping included in this volume will help the VSE focus on relevant information to adopt and adapt. Information in the International Standards community gives an audit path for the VSE, allowing them to demonstrate compliance with globally agreed requirements, which creates possible commercial opportunities. Although the Five Anchors were not mapped specifically to the frameworks, they help determine which improvement tool is the most applicable to the organization. For the VSE, this creates a level of expediency and efficiency to support their service delivery. Once the benefit is realized, the VSE may be able to find the resources to pursue full compliance if helpful to the business.

CHAPTER 4: THE FIVE ANCHORS

Before we dive into the caselets, there is a core set of information applied to each caselet which guides a potential "solution." We call this framework the **Five Anchors** and it revolves around a series of 15 questions in five key areas. These questions (numbered below) allow you to focus on fundamental management areas from an enterprise perspective. Each question is further expanded in the bullets. The breadth of these questions allow the user to look "full scope" rather than risking a constrained focus (e.g. the stereotypic knee-jerk reaction towards technology solutions).

The Five Anchors

I. Strategic Alignment: IT Services to Business Objectives

1. What are the business strategy, goals and objectives?
   What are the measures that demonstrate the achievement of the business strategy, goals and objectives?
   o This information should be gathered *before* any improvement initiative begins so the solution to the issue is based on business need. *Additionally, measures (CSFs, KPIs) should be defined, understood and deployed at this point in order to create the necessary baseline to show improvements.*

2. What is the business issue or activity at risk?
   o Is a vital business function at risk, is it a new market activity, or is there a high degree of urgency and/or impact (priority)?

3. Is the ownership to resolve the situation (caselet scenario) at the appropriate level of authority?
   o The solution set or current situation should be addressed by an accountable named role, therefore, is that role the decision-authority?

II.   **Security, Compliance and Risk Issues**
1. Has there been a compromise of the information security policy?
   - Review the confidentiality, integrity and accessibility of information resources and ensure the business issue has not breached the approved and/or agreed information security policy (protect business interest).
2. What are the internal and external compliance or regulatory concerns?
   - Apply an appropriate balance among the relevant regulatory, statutory and contractual obligations to ensure business outcomes are met (performance and conformance).
3. What is the cultural appetite for risk?
   - Define and agree with key stakeholders the organizational risk tolerance, understanding that risk tolerance may differ among departments, services, entities, etc.

III.   **Value-based Portfolio**
1. Does the current portfolio meet expectations and needs of the stakeholder?
   - Does the service provider have the necessary resources and capabilities to create the necessary level of customer satisfaction (business outcomes, preferences and perceptions)?
2. What is the value of the affected business activity (VBF)?
   - Use the outcome of a Business Impact Analysis (BIA), SWOT analysis (Strengths, Weaknesses, Opportunities, Threats), PESTEL analysis (Political, Economic, Social, Technological, Environmental, Legal), etc., to understand the impact of the situation and classify appropriately. If we understand the value and impact of the activity in terms of the business need, we can deploy the correct resources and capability.
3. Does the portfolio have the right mix of resources to deliver business benefit?
   - Link portfolio resources to the defined IT and business strategies to ensure ROI/VOI. This entails balancing the appropriate investment mix which links current strategies to financial resources.

IV. Design and Architecture

1. Will the current architecture effectively resolve the situation? Is it feasible?
   o Define the current architectural layers (i.e. business process, information, data, application, technology) and are those layers feasible to support the current situation?
2. Can the current architecture accommodate the situation?
   o Is the current architecture flexible, scalable, available, reliable, resilient, usable, maintainable, secure, affordable, etc.?
3. Do we have the necessary competencies to design the required change(s)?
   o Do current staff, internal or consultants, have the necessary skills, knowledge, information and experience or expertise to meet the design requirements?

V. Planning and Use of Resources

1. What resources are required to resolve the situation (e.g. people, capital, technical...)?
   o Begin the planning process and list all potential resources to resolve the situation – think from an idyllic perspective and then let organizational constraints filter that list to an acceptable solution set.
2. Can the required resources be acquired?
   o Evaluate current resource capability toward meeting desired objectives versus a procured external solution ("build vs. buy").
3. Is the necessary data and information available, collected and managed to resolve the current situation and prevent future occurrence?
   o Is information managed from creation to retirement?

Structure

In the following chapters, we present ten unique caselets that represent common issues in the following general areas:

- Governance
- Resource optimization
- Risk Management

- Achievement of business outcomes
- Compliance and/or Improvement
- Strategic Alignment
- Security, Compliance & Risk
- Value-based Portfolio
- Strategic Choice & Market Conditions
- Planning & Use of Resources.

In each of the caselets, we have applied the Five Anchors to chart an improvement course and documented our thoughts based on the caselet details. If appropriate, we have listed sections from COBIT, ISO/IEC 20000, ITIL and CMMI-SVC that would support or clarify the situation. For CMMI-SVC, we have added only PAs up to level 3 and left out PAs at levels 4 or 5. We have used section numbers only for clarity – major section numbers have been provided in tables in the preceding chapters. Lastly, based on the analysis, we have applied one of the improvement models and defined the key steps required for successful resolution.

CHAPTER 5:
CASELET #1 - GOVERNANCE

IT Issue: An international import/export company is expecting significant growth over the next two years. The Board of Directors recently held a two-day retreat, during which they created an IT Governance Committee. This was in response to the growing reliance on IT systems, their interoperability and the overall past performance of the IT organization. The IT Governance Committee met for the first time last month and convened with the following areas that needed further study:

- What vital business processes are dependent on IT and what are their requirements?
- How much of the IT effort is spent on fighting fires rather than enabling the business?
- Do we have sufficient IT resources and infrastructure to meet the strategic objectives of the business?
- Have we addressed all non-minor IT-related risks?

The VP of IT has been asked to create a presentation for the next IT Governance Committee meeting to address the above concerns and suggest action plans to address any shortcomings or gaps.

The Five Anchors

Anchor	Discussion
I. Strategic Alignment: IT Services to Business Objectives	
1. What are the business strategy, goals and objectives? *Are there any measures that demonstrate the achievement of the business strategy, goals and objectives?*	• No matter what the business issue or scenario you're trying to improve, you *must* always know the business strategy, goals and objectives. If you do not have a process in place that drives IT activity through business

Anchor	Discussion
	strategy, goals and objectives, review: • **COBIT**: Goals Cascade • **CMMI-SVC**: STSM; SSD SG1; WP SG1 • **ISO20K**: Implied through the fulfillment of service requirements (4.0) • **ITIL**: SS 4.1, 5.1.1; SD 3.1.6, 3.5; CSI 3.10
2. What is the business issue, or activity at risk?	• In order to meet the projected growth, IT systems must change their philosophy and design parameters to meet the new business requirements not only for the growth but also resilience and security concerns. • **COBIT**: Goals Cascade, EDM3 • **CMMI-SVC**: SSD • **ISO20K**: 4.0, 6.3, 6.5, 6.6 • **ITIL**: SD 4.4, 4.5, 4.7
3. Is the ownership to resolve the issue at the appropriate level of authority?	• While the VP of IT has been tasked with the reporting, we can assume also tasked with the responsibility and/or accountability that the necessary changes are made. We do not have enough information to confirm this action. • What we do know is that the Board created a Governance Committee who has delegated the responsibility of resolving the situation to the IT leadership which is consistent with the COBIT enabler "Organizational Structures."

Anchor	Discussion
	• **CMMI-SVC**: OPF; GPs 2.4, 2.10
II. Security, Compliance and Risk Issues	
1. Has there been a compromise of the information security policy?	• N/A
2. What are the internal and external compliance or regulatory concerns?	• As an international import/export company, we can assume there are regulatory, legal and perhaps contractual obligations. As a general rule, we would ensure these constraints would be considered and mitigated in any improvement design. • **COBIT**: APO11, MEA3 • **CMMI-SVC**: SSD SG1; OPF SG 1
3. What is the cultural appetite for risk?	• Because there is active executive involvement by the Board, there is an understanding that IT risks be documented and addressed. A specific request for plans around addressing all IT-related risks is an outcome, therefore, even though it is not stated in the caselet, the assumption is low risk tolerance. • **COBIT**: EDM3, APO12 • **CMMI-SVC**: RSKM; GP 2.10 • **ITIL**: SS 5.6.5, D.3, E
III. Value-based Portfolio	
1. Does the current portfolio meet expectations and	• Assumed, yes; but will the current portfolio meet the needs of the future business direction? • **COBIT**: APOAPO5 • **CMMI-SVC**: STSM SG 1

Anchor	Discussion
needs of the stakeholder?	• **ISO20K**: 5.0 • **ITIL**: SS 4.2
2. What is the value of the affected business activity (VBF)?	• While there is not a specific service described, the overall activities of IT must meet the future growth, security and availability needs. • Review "Strategic Alignment", question #2 above
3. Does the portfolio have the right mix of resources to deliver business benefit?	• The assumption is "yes" because outsourcing has not been mentioned by the Governance Committee. That doesn't mean in the report by the VP of IT, in answering the Committee's concerns, that outsourcing is not an option for consideration in meeting future requirements. • **COBIT**: EDM2, EDM4, APO5 • **CMMI-SVC**: SSD; STSM SG1 • **ITIL**: SS 3.7; SD 3.11
IV. Design and Architecture	
1. Will the current architecture effectively resolve the issue? Is it feasible?	• This issue must be addressed to meet the utility and warranty needs of the organization. The current architecture appears to effectively meet the needs now, but given the planned growth, a detailed assessment is required to ensure support of future business strategy. Data and information gathered from Technical and Application Management teams provide the necessary input. • **COBIT**: APO3 • **CMMI-SVC**: SSD

Anchor	Discussion
	• **ITIL**: SO 6.4, 6.6
2. Can the current architecture accommodate the issue?	• At this point, no information to the contrary is available. • **CMMI-SVC**: SSD SG2; SCON SG3
3. Do we have the necessary competencies to design the required change(s)?	• VP of IT is responsible for the response to the Governance Committee. There is no definite indication in the caselet that the necessary competencies are not available. • **CMMI-SVC**: SSD; SD SG2; SP 2.5
V. Planning and Use of Resources	
1. What resources are required to resolve the situation (e.g. people, capital, technical...)?	• Unknown with the information provided.
2. Can the required resources be acquired?	• N/A but assuming the support is available if only through the enterprise-based questions from the Governance Committee and recognition of increased reliance on IT systems.
3. Is the necessary data and information available, collected and managed to resolve the current situation and prevent future occurrence?	• Unknown with the information provided.

Improvement Model Application

This scenario can be resolved by following any of the four improvement models but we will focus on just two: ITIL's CSI Approach and COBIT's Implementation Model. This caselet demands a review of what is currently in place and then an examination of the gap between now and what is needed. If we focus on the first three steps of the CSI Approach and COBIT's Implementation Model, we effectively ensure we address the organization strategies, goals and objectives and capture an unbiased view of "now" and clearly delineate the gap to the "future."

Solution References:

Primary Solution:

COBIT: The main source of information will come from the Goals Cascade and two domains: EDM and APO. But, to get to those domains and processes, we strongly encourage you to utilize the Goals Cascade, which can be found in *COBIT 5: A Business Framework for the Governance and Management of Enterprise IT* (pg. 18). The Goals Cascade directly relates to Principle 1 "Meeting Stakeholder Needs" which is a foremost concern in this caselet. The *Business Framework* document is not member-only information and can be freely downloaded at *www.isaca.org*.

To summarize how the goals cascade flows, the general steps to conduct in this exercise include:

- Understanding the stakeholder drivers and map them to stakeholder needs
- Cascade stakeholder needs to Enterprise Goals
- Cascade Enterprise Goals to IT-Related Goals
- Cascade IT-related Goals to Enabler Goals
- Determine appropriate processes (particularly from the EDM and APO domains).

Secondary Solution

CMMI-SVC has capabilities associated with strategic analysis of the business and cascades them into the enterprise service system. CMMI-SVC also has practices associated with establishing, maintaining and monitoring a risk management system for the service. Elements of this model should be reviewed to enhance the overall solution.

ISO/IEC 20000 and ITIL are underpinned by the need for overall governance and risk management, but neither has defined risk management processes or governance mandates. Both frameworks address these elements at different levels and from different perspectives, therefore directing us to use COBIT as the primary solution. Elements from these models should be reviewed and incorporated as needed to resolve the situation based on the culture and environment to the organization. We have listed areas within the Five Anchors discussion that point you to specific references. We will not repeat them here.

CHAPTER 6:
CASELET #2 - RESOURCE OPTIMIZATION

IT Issue: A managed service provider delivers outsourced IT services for mid-market companies primarily in the manufacturing sector. This is a multi-tenant provider with two primary data centres. Reacting to a market opportunity identified by the Board nine months ago, this company hastily launched a new major SaaS offering in order to gain market share.

The company conducted a vendor selection for the core functionality and contracted with multiple consultants to complete the customization required to provide the value-add aspects of the new service. Many key resources were reassigned to the new effort with little backfilling. In an effort to save costs, many infrastructure decisions were deferred, opting to simply use as much of the current infrastructure capacity as possible to support the rollout. There was very little demand planning used to understand usage patterns or growth estimates.

Since the launch of the new service, multiple issues have surfaced:

- Customers have complained that the performance of the service is slow and the user experience is poor.
- Tier one support staff are overwhelmed with issues and requests that cannot be resolved at their level and must be escalated to the vendor, resulting in missed service levels.
- Other key areas of the IT function are understaffed due to the reassignment of key talent to support the SaaS launch, causing customer complaints in areas that were previously efficient.

The Five Anchors

Anchor	Discussion
I. Strategic Alignment: IT Services to Business Objectives	
1. What are the business strategy, goals and objectives? *Are there any measures that demonstrate the achievement of the business strategy, goals and objectives?*	• From a high-level, this organization is trying to gain market share as quickly as possible by launching SaaS services. This is a classic example of "Shoot, Shoot, Shoot, Ready, Aim." There really is no definite strategy for these actions. Obviously some sort of a management system is needed as well as a concerted effort to define and control actions. • **COBIT**: APO2 • **CMMI-SVC**: CAM; IRP SG 3 • **ISO20K**: Implied through the fulfillment of service requirements (4.0) • **ITIL**: SS 3.4, 4.1; SD 3.5
2. What is the business issue, or activity at risk?	• The very real threat is to the ongoing service delivery and customer satisfaction. Worst scenario, this managed service provider is at risk for continued solvency. • **CMMI-SVC**: SD; CAM
3. Is the ownership to resolve the issue at the appropriate level of authority?	• Unknown with the information provided. • **CMMI-SVC**: GP 2.4

Anchor	Discussion
II. Security, Compliance and Risk Issues	
1. Has there been a compromise of the information security policy?	• The threat is very real, but it is unknown. We may be able to assume that since there have been no security incidents, that this is not a major factor. More data and information would be necessary to definitively answer this question.
2. What are the internal and external compliance or regulatory concerns?	• This is a multi-tenant service provider with multiple contracts. We do not know the type of service or level of regulatory controls (i.e. PCI/DSS, HIPPA, SOX, SSAE, etc.) but we would certainly address those legal and/or statutory requirements or other contractual obligations to provide a scope of operations for the improvement efforts. • **COBIT**: MEA2, MEA3 • **CMMI-SVC**: SSD SG1; OPF SG 1
3. What is the cultural appetite for risk?	• Obviously it's recklessly high and perhaps management needs to step back a bit and redefine their service delivery and management to better fit the SaaS environment. • **COBIT**: EDM3 • **CMMI-SVC**: RSKM SG 1
III. Value-based Portfolio	
1. Does the current portfolio meet expectations and	• At this point, the answer is "No" and it is based on customer feedback and staffing issues. This

Anchor	Discussion
needs of the stakeholder?	is an area that needs defined improvements. • **COBIT**: EDM2, APO5 • **CMMI-SVC**: STSM SG 1 • **ISO20K**: 4.4, 7.1 • **ITIL**: SS 3.5, 4.2, 4.5; SD 3.4, 3.5
2. What is the value of the affected business activity (VBF)?	• It is their line of business, thus this SaaS service requires absolute control and management.
3. Does the portfolio have the right mix of resources to deliver business benefit?	• At this point in time, perhaps, but they are not being managed or optimized for customer or service provider benefit. Management needs to define the necessary level of competencies to support the SaaS service as well the other services in their catalog. Appropriate relationship management with the customer needs to be improved (e.g. relationship managers, better training, better information on the new service, etc.). • **COBIT**: EDM4, APO7, APO8 • **CMMI-SVC**: SSD • **ISO20K**: 4.1, 4.4, 7.1 • **ITIL**: SS 4.5, SD 4.5, 6.5, C.12
IV. Design and Architecture	
1. Will the current architecture effectively resolve the issue? Is it feasible?	• No. The current architecture did not consider any forecasted demand which is causing the current issues. Therefore, logically, new plans to support the SaaS service as well as improve the delivery of all services to restore customer

Anchor	Discussion
	confidence and satisfaction must be developed and deployed. • **COBIT**: APO3, APO9, APO10, BAI4 • **CMMI-SVC**: SSD; CAM; MA • **ISO20K**: 6.1, 6.3, 6.5, 7.2 • **ITIL**: SD 3.4, 3.5, 4.1, 4.3, 4.4, 4.5, 4.8; ST 4.2
2. Can the current architecture accommodate the issue?	• No, see directly above.
3. Do we have the necessary competencies to design the required change(s)?	• Unknown – staff were moved to address the new initiative and external consultants were also used. Knowledge transfer did not occur nor were staff backfilled when they were moved. A serious look must be made around the necessary resources to continue to deliver all services. • **COBIT**: APO7 • **CMMI-SVC**: SSD SG 2; OT; GP 2.5 • **ISO20K**: 4.4, 4.5.2, 4.5.3, 5.2, 5.3 • **ITIL**: SD 4.5, 6.5, N.12 • **SFIA** (*www.sfia-online.org*): SFIA is an internationally accepted framework around skills and competencies within IT, matching areas of work to levels of responsibility. It is a wonderful tool for organizational skills management.
V. Planning and Use of Resources	

Anchor	Discussion
1. What resources are required to resolve the situation (e.g. people, capital, technical...)?	• A full review of all resources (e.g. people, capital, technical, etc.) is required. • **COBIT**: APO7 • **CMMI-SVC**: SSD • **ISO20K**: 4.4 • **ITIL**: SD 4.5; ST 4.2
2. Can the required resources be acquired?	• Of course. To ensure efficiency and economics, competencies and an accurate technical design are required *BEFORE* resources are procured. • **COBIT**: APO7 • **CMMI-SVC**: SSD • **ISO20K**: 4.4, 4.5.2, 4.5.3, 5.2, 5.3 • **ITIL**: SD 4.5
3. Is the necessary data and information available, collected and managed to resolve the current situation and prevent future occurrence?	• We certainly know what's wrong, but now we need to act in an efficient, effective and economic manner. The "shoot from the hip" actions that created the SaaS service must be curtailed and a process to support all services and service provider activities must be created. • **COBIT**: BAI8, Information Enabler • **CMMI-SVC**: IRP SG 3 • **ITIL**: ST 4.7; CSI 3.9

Improvement Model Application

Deming's PDCA comes to mind immediately in this situation – planning was omitted and now there are definite issues. To correct, the plans to support the SaaS service, as well as the remaining service catalogue, must be created to ensure not only the technology is addressed – address staff competencies as well as their roles and responsibility. Deploy (do) this plan in an organized and controlled fashion to mitigate impact on current service delivery (as bad as it is – don't make it worse!). Lastly, as plans are developed, ensure there are quality measures (check) in place to enable clear reporting on the performance of the services from a technology and a customer satisfaction view. Act on those reports and deploy improvements as needed.

ISO/IEC 20000-1:2011 and ISO/IEC 20000-2:2012 offer clear and concise guidance around PDCA. Additionally, this information is coupled with the overall concept of a service management system, further reinforcing the need to clearly define leadership roles, policies and communication. *Design and transition of new and changed services* (Clause 5) offers a high-level overview of moving from a concept to an operational service in production. These activities are clearly under the control of Change Management highlighting the need for a strong Change Management process – not Change Scheduling! Clauses 5.2-5.4 provide the areas for consideration not only for the development of the plan and supporting policies for the SaaS service, but also the activities for design, development and transition.

Solution References:

Primary Solution:

ISO20K: *Establish and Improve the SMS* (4.5) definitively details the PDCA actions required for ongoing management and improvement of the SMS. Consider each area, analyse its efficacy within the organization and define an improvement program.

Secondary Solution:

ITIL: Within the pages of *ITIL Service Design*, the Five Aspects of Service Design (service solution, management information systems, technology, architectures and tools, processes and measures and metrics) provide a technological view of a new or changed service. These aspects are supported by the processes listed above with a direct concentration on overall management

(DC) as well as the remaining design-oriented processes (AM, CapM, ITSCM, ISM, SuppM).

COBIT: Confirm the objectives via the Goals Cascade and review the information around APO7 and BAI8. Incorporate the relevant pieces into the improvement plans.

CMMI-SVC: Business goals are defined and confirmed within STSM. Any improvement or change to the SMS is planned, monitored and managed through SSD.

CHAPTER 7:
CASELET #3 - RISK MANAGEMENT

IT Issue: A candy manufacturer conducted a selection process for a major ERP replacement system. The implementation was supposed to be completed within nine months. At the seven-month mark of the implementation, it was determined that the effort would need to be extended. The Executive Steering Committee remained strangely silent during the decision-making process and very little effort was made by the program team to identify risks (i.e. incompatible architectural components, data migration issues, poor transition plans, etc.) and develop meaningful strategies to deal with those risks. With a major holiday approaching, the manufacturer is now expediting the implementation by adding more resources to the team with the intent of meeting the original nine-month timeframe and of not impacting the major sales season.

The addition of the extra resources was the solution necessary to meet the original timeframe. The implementation was completed following a 'big bang' approach just two months before the busiest holiday season of the year. Unfortunately, the implementation caused a widespread system outage and required a complete release back-out. The company's only choice at this point was to utilize the old systems. This created a massive backlog of manufacturing orders, unhappy angry customers and lost orders.

The Five Anchors

Anchor	Discussion
I. Strategic Alignment: IT Services to Business Objectives	
1. What are the business strategy, goals and objectives?	• While every organization will have some strategy defined, we don't know what it is here.

Anchor	Discussion
Are there any measures that demonstrate the achievement of the business strategy, goals and objectives?	Know that any solution should link to the achievement of the enterprise strategy, goals and objectives.
2. What is the business issue, or activity at risk?	• Production and shipment of the organization's product line during peak sales season. • **CMMI-SVC**: SCON
3. Is the ownership to resolve the issue at the appropriate level of authority?	• Unknown, but the Executive Steering Committee for some unknown reason went silent during a crucial IT decision. Where is Change Management? • **CMMI-SVC**: GG2
II. Security, Compliance and Risk Issues	
1. Has there been a compromise of the information security policy?	• Unknown with the information provided.
2. What are the internal and external compliance or regulatory concerns?	• Certainly there are regulatory or compliance issues that need to be addressed. The main issue though is the contractual obligations with the customer.
3. What is the cultural appetite for risk?	• We assume there is discussion around the underpinning environment but the Executive Steering Committee (and any Change Management system) certainly ignored any known corporate culture for risk. • **COBIT**: APO12, BAI6 • **CMMI-SVC**: SST; SCON

Anchor	Discussion
	• **ISO20K**: 4.1, 4.5.2, 4.5.3, 5.2, 6.3 • **ITIL**: SD 4.4, 4.6, 4.7, M, N.3; ST 4.2, 4.6
III. Value-based Portfolio	
1. Does the current portfolio meet expectations and needs of the stakeholder?	• Unknown with the information provided.
2. What is the value of the affected business activity (VBF)?	• This is their core business. Without this system, product is not being shipped therefore the potential and probability for sales and customer loss is high. • **CMMI-SVC**: SCON; IRP
3. Does the portfolio have the right mix of resources to deliver business benefit?	• Assuming yes; the target delivery date was met, there were no other indications of failure or poor performance (other than the future massive failure).
IV. Design and Architecture	
1. Will the current architecture effectively resolve the issue? Is it feasible?	• Unknown with the information provided. • **CMMI-SVC**: SSD
2. Can the current architecture accommodate the issue?	• Unknown with the information provided. • **CMMI-SVC**: SSD

Anchor	Discussion
3. Do we have the necessary competencies to design the required change(s)?	• The assumption is yes. The current staff were able to meet the deadline and deal with all the moving parts of deploying a new ERP system. What was lacking was a thoughtful assessment of what could go wrong and have mitigating plans prepared. • **CMMI-SVC**: SSD; SST
V. Planning and Use of Resources	
1. What resources are required to resolve the situation (e.g. people, capital, technical…)?	• Better project planning where exceptions are considered and a more realistic view of time and resource necessary for the roll-out. This could have been accomplished by a better charter within the Executive Steering Group where proper oversight is forefront as well as their demand of the project team to report progress appropriately. • **COBIT**: EDM3, APO12, BAI1, BAI3, BAI6, BAI7 • **CMMI-SVC**: SSD; SST; SCON; WMC; WP • **ISO20K**: 5.0 • **ITIL**: ST 4.2, 4.4, 4.5, 4.6
2. Can the required resources be acquired?	• The assumption would be yes.
3. Is the necessary data and information available, collected and managed to resolve the current	• Unknown with the information provided.

Anchor	Discussion
situation and prevent future occurrence?	

Improvement Model Application

This scenario really falls into an "esoteric" category – it points directly at understanding the organizational tolerance toward risk, having the management leadership to control how projects are performed and having a robust Change Management process. It's really a cultural issue where process has not been designed (followed?) to ensure minimal impact of change. There are many process areas where one could focus; the main culprits are the overall management system, governance and Change Management.

The main improvement model would be COBIT's Implementation Model – Phase 1 of this model "What are the drivers?" includes a failed IT initiative among others (e.g. internal or external events, trends, poor performance, etc.). The main outcome of Phase 1 is the development of a business case written for the executive management level and this case will be managed and monitored to ensure a successful outcome. This would have been of great use to the Executive Steering Committee in guiding their actions and decisions.

The tangible application of the Implementation Model comes in Phase 2, "Where are we now?", which links IT objectives with enterprise strategies and risks. This linkage defines the critical processes necessary for successful outcomes. Now we have a defined objective, clearly linking the necessary IT capabilities with the achievement of business outcome. This very action should have provided the necessary governance and oversight so that some of the "cowboy" activities would have been curtailed.

The underpinning policy in any service management framework is the control by the change management process. ISO/IEC 20000-1 unequivocally states the process of design and transition of new or changed services shall be managed via the change management policy and process. Period. The ultimate in control, at least as long as the process is robust enough and followed. If it's not, well, that's another issue that must be addressed and quickly (and in a different book!).

Solution References:

Primary Solution

Both COBIT and ISO/IEC 20000-1 drive the service manager to understand the risk appetite and then define and mitigate risk within those parameters. The SMS and the principles defined in the design and transition process demand it and manage those via Change Management. COBIT has defined specific processes around risk (APO12) and change (BAI6) to ensure the intended outcome is achieved.

CMMI-SVC is particularly strong in examining resource needs, design and development, whether initial or ongoing during change and in planning, monitoring and adjusting to ongoing service needs.

Secondary Solution

ITIL: All ST processes, especially "true" Change Management, control risk. Change Evaluation evaluates the benefits of a new or changed service from the "as planned/to be delivered" perspective and reports not only on the achievement of service requirements but also risk (specifically, residual risk). Their recommendations are submitted to Change Management for consideration in the "go/no-go" decision at key points in the transition cycle.

CHAPTER 8:
CASELET #4 – ACHIEVE BUSINESS OUTCOMES

IT Issue: A small auto insurance company has experienced significant growth in the last several years. The IT department has done a good job of managing increasing capacity requirements based on the demand patterns. Additionally, they provide an onsite service desk as well as level 2 and level 3 support and a fairly active PMO. In a strategic planning session held last year, the company leadership made it very clear that there were three vital areas which the IT department needed to focus on: 1) communication technologies must have high availability, 2) downtime of critical services must be kept to a minimum and 3) customers need a self-help portal that provides value.

The IT department deployed all of the necessary technologies to support the stated vital needs of the business (as well as continued support of the core business functions), but continually had issues around supporting those services. The following issues have been identified in the last six months:

- The self-help portal doesn't provide information for the most commonly used services.
  - o It is rarely used due to a poor design.
- Incident and request ticket backlog has grown by 120%.
- Three major incidents have occurred resulting in large amounts of downtime to critical services; one failure caused a 12-hour outage within their mobile communication technologies.

The Five Anchors

Anchor	Discussion
I. Strategic Alignment: IT Services to Business Objectives	
1. What are the business strategy, goals and objectives? *Are there any measures that demonstrate the achievement of the business strategy, goals and objectives?*	• The continued growth of the business is paramount but no specific business goals or objectives have been stated. What has been communicated is that IT must provide high availability, reduce the downtime of the critical services (implying the creation or improvement of a continuity plan) and provide a method of self-help. No measures are mentioned but could be easily created as necessary. • **CMMI-SVC**: CAM; MA
2. What is the business issue, or activity at risk?	• There are two issues – first the downtime of the critical services, which needs to be addressed not only from an agreed delivery position (i.e. SLAs and appropriate availability requirements and planning) but also from the intangible cost perspectives (i.e. confidence, reputation, etc.) all of which can lead to a loss of customers. Big question: Is there an IT Service Continuity plan? The second issue is one of poor support (backlog of incident and request tickets as well as major incidents). • **COBIT**: BAI4

Anchor	Discussion
	• **CMMI-SVC**: SD SG1; CAM; SCON; IRP • **ISO20K**: 5.0, 6.3, 6.5 • **ITIL**: SD 4.4, 4.5, 4.6
3. Is the ownership to resolve the issue at the appropriate level of authority?	• Unclear, though organizational leadership did communicate what IT was to accomplish – we do not know the roles within IT but could assume a "like" position or direct report to the company leadership received those requests and then assigned as appropriate. • **CMMI-SVC**: GPs 2.4, 2.10
II. Security, Compliance and Risk Issues	
1. Has there been a compromise of the information security policy?	• Unknown with the information provided.
2. What are the internal and external compliance or regulatory concerns?	• There are regulatory concerns within auto insurance companies, but the caselet does not hint that there have been any issues. But, this is a constraint for any planning of new or changed services to ensure continued compliance to the internal or external regulatory concerns or contractual obligations. • **COBIT**: APO11, MEA3 • **CMMI-SVC**: SSD SG1; OPF SG 1
3. What is the cultural appetite for risk?	• The organization has experienced growth and we've assumed they do want to continue that pattern. Logically, one can make a case

Anchor	Discussion
	that the strong growth pattern is a result of taking some risks to gain market share, thus the organization may be willing to accept some level of risk.
III. Value-based Portfolio	
1. Does the current portfolio meet expectations and needs of the stakeholder?	• The portfolio meets the needs of the organization if only due to the successful growth. The issues now seem to revolve around operational demand and support and the lack of a continuity plan (remember the 12-hour outage). IT should be analyzing the trends of use, develop/improve a continuity plan and ensure appropriate knowledge and resources for the design and support staff. • **CMMI-SVC**: SSD; CAM
2. What is the value of the affected business activity (VBF)?	• For the auto insurance industry, communication is vital for new policies, claims and policy management. The outages within communication technology directly affect the viability of this company. This IT organization would benefit from completing a Business Impact Analysis (BIA), if it hasn't been done already, to quantify and qualify the impact of the IT service loss. • **CMMI-SVC**: SCON • **ITIL**: SD 4.6.5.2 (BIA)
3. Does the portfolio have the right mix of resources to deliver business benefit?	• Logically, we have to assume yes, if only because of the growth that has been managed to date (i.e. necessary

Anchor	Discussion
	functionality has been delivered). The current issues are more support process-oriented, rather than a non-functional service, specifically around the backlog of incidents and requests as well as the under-used and poorly designed self-help portal. • **CMMI-SVC**: SSD
IV. Design and Architecture	
1. Will the current architecture effectively resolve the issue? Is it feasible?	• In the balancing of resources and capabilities, we assume they have the resources but capabilities may be lacking (i.e. management, processes, knowledge, organization and people). The current self-help portal is obviously not effective, thus requiring a major change. It is assumed the IT organization will require additional resources and capabilities for that project. • **CMMI-SVC**: SSD
2. Can the current architecture accommodate the issue?	• There is no evidence the current architecture cannot overcome the issues.
3. Do we have the necessary competencies to design the required change(s)?	• Unknown at this point – but there are two pertinent facts: 1) IT has been able to keep up with the capacity demands; 2) IT has done a very poor job in designing a self-help system. Thus, IT leadership should define and re-examine current competencies, especially around the support

Anchor	Discussion
	area and improve where necessary. • **COBIT**: APO7 • **CMMI-SVC**: SSD; GP 2.5 • **ISO20K**: 4.4 • **ITIL**: SS 6.10, SD 6.5, ST 6.6, SO 6.9, CSI 6.6 • **SFIA** (*www.sfia-online.org*)
V. Planning and Use of Resources	
1. What resources are required to resolve the situation (e.g. people, capital, technical...)?	• Clearly, this IT organization needs to take a strong look at their support processes as well as the flexibility and continuity of their designs to address continued demand and mitigate the outages. Resource management practices need a review – has the company growth exceeded IT capacity? Additionally, a knowledge base for the self-help portal requires development and on-going maintenance for applicability. • **COBIT**: BAI4, BAI8, DSS2, DSS4 • **CMMI-SVC**: SSD; CAM; SST • **ISO20K**: 4.4., 4.5, 5.0, 6.3, 8.1 • **ITIL**: SD 4.4, 4.6; ST 4.7; SO 4.2
2. Can the required resources be acquired?	• Without a doubt. The organizational sourcing model is unknown but current technologies are available to resolve the issues as long as this organization clearly defines the requirements before engaging a commercial solution (e.g. outsource the service desk,

Anchor	Discussion
	commercial tools to create the self-help portal, etc.). • **COBIT**: APO10 • **CMMI-SVC**: SSD; SAM • **ISO20K**: 7.2 • **ITIL**: SS 3.7, SD 3.11, 4.8
3. Is the necessary data and information available, collected and managed to resolve the current situation and prevent future occurrence?	• Clearly, there is some data available as we know of the poor use of the self-help portal, backlogs and outages. Is it being used to create a solution and or prevent future occurrence? That is unknown. • **COBIT**: Information Enabler • **CMMI-SVC**: IRP SG 3 • **ISO20K**: 6.2 • **ITIL**: CSI 4.1

Improvement Model Application

This entire scenario screams "Process improvement!" and ITIL's CSI Approach and Seven-Step Improvement process would be an excellent fit to effectively and efficiently guide the necessary improvements. It is obvious the current practices are not keeping up with current business requirements and damaging overall business operations. To apply the CSI Approach, confirmation of organizational goals and objectives is necessary ("What is the vision?") as well as a clearly defined future state ("Where do we want to be?") *before* the development of process and service improvements ("How do we get there?"). Remember, this organization already has some measures for its current state (we will not make a value judgment if those measures are sufficient).

These steps clearly relate to the Seven-Step Improvement Process, which really focuses on the collection of appropriate data to support improvement efforts. This process demands a very clear structure around the whole activity of data collection and analysis creating repeatable measures which drives reliability. Deploying this process would serve the organization well - if they are to continue to grow, developing consistency around the information upon which decisions are made, will serve them well.

Solution References:

Primary Solution:

ISO20K and ITIL: Review the requirements for Incident and Service Request Management (8.1) defined in ISO/IEC 20000-1 and consider the other practices described in ITIL around incidents and service requests. Also, review the clear and concise process in ISO/IEC 20000-1 for the design and transition of new or changed services (it can be applied to process improvement as well) and go back and "fill in" the missing parts to create a better self-help portal as well as critically review the availability designs. ITIL offers expanded information in several areas:

- SD 3.0, 4.4; SO 4.2, 4.3; CSI 4.1

As recommended above, strongly consider the review and update of IT staff competencies and invest in their continued growth. SFIA offers a globally accepted framework for defining the various roles and competencies.

Secondary Solution:

Utilize the information within COBIT (as listed above) to guide metric development as well as appropriate relationships and communication between processes and stakeholders utilizing the RACI diagrams.

CHAPTER 9:
CASELET #5 – COMPLIANCE & IMPROVEMENT

IT Issue: Last year, in an effort to get better visibility of assets in the company, a publicly traded energy company created a small IT team to manage the PC asset register. The intent of the team was to document the acquisition of PCs and assign ownership to each. Additionally, the software installed on each PC was managed via a software licensing contract ensuring up-to-date versions. This contract also documented the number of licenses distributed throughout the energy company for billing purposes.

In a recent internal asset audit, the team discovered that out of the 3000 PCs in the register, 300 had not been on the network in the last nine months (most of these were laptops) and it was unknown who had them or their locations. Upon learning this, the IT Director quickly held a meeting in which the following concerns were raised:

- It is unknown whether the 300 PCs have been lost, stolen, or simply being used in the field without having connected to the company's network.
- Sensitive information could be on the PCs.
- Since these have not been on the network in the last nine months, their anti-virus software could be out of date.
- The company is paying for licenses on PCs that are not being used.

The Five Anchors

Anchor	Discussion
I. Strategic Alignment: IT Services to Business Objectives	
1. What are the business strategy, goals and objectives? *Are there any measures that*	• Unknown with the information provided.

Anchor	Discussion
demonstrate the achievement of the business strategy, goals and objectives?	
2. What is the business issue, or activity at risk?	• Truly this an asset management issue. This organization has "lost" 10% of the purchased (or leased?) PCs and the impact is far beyond the actual physical device. There should be concerns around corporate data (data confidentiality), actual loss of corporate property and payment of license and potential maintenance fees. • **CMMI-SVC**: CM
3. Is the ownership to resolve the issue at the appropriate level of authority?	• The IT Director is now aware of the issue and it would be presumed there would be an appropriate delegation of this issue with the IT Director continuing in the accountable role.
II. Security, Compliance and Risk Issues	
1. Has there been a compromise of the information security policy?	• While the caselet doesn't directly state this is an issue, the possibility is very real. • **COBIT**: APO13, BAI9, DSS5 • **CMMI-SVC**: SM • **ISO20K**: 6.6, 9.1 • **ITIL**: SD 4.7; ST 4.3
2. What are the internal and external compliance or regulatory concerns?	• As a publicly traded company, there are numerous regulatory, statutory and legal concerns (as well as potential contractual obligations). A primary concern

Anchor	Discussion
	within a majority of the regulations includes positive control of company information assets (i.e. safeguarding of customer information, etc.). • **COBIT**: APO11, MEA3 • **CMMI-SVC**: OPF; GG 2 • **ISO20K**: 4.1 • **ITIL**: 4.1
3. What is the cultural appetite for risk?	• The nature of the organization would presume a low risk appetite in some areas and others (trading) may have a much higher appetite. What is important to know from an IT perspective and for this specific issue, is understanding what potential information and services are at risk and the overall vulnerability to the energy company. • **CMMI-SVC**: RSKM
III. Value-based Portfolio	
1. Does the current portfolio meet expectations and needs of the stakeholder?	• Unknown with the information provided.
2. What is the value of the affected business activity (VBF)?	• Unknown with the information provided.
3. Does the portfolio have the right mix of resources to deliver business benefit?	• Unknown with the information provided.

Anchor	Discussion
IV. Design and Architecture	
1. Will the current architecture effectively resolve the issue? Is it feasible?	• The process architecture demands improvement. There seems to be some level of control of the infrastructure and there is no indication of outage or compromise. But, the issue clearly is one of asset management and the lack of process that will maintain control over corporate assets. • Therefore, the IT Director (or delegate to an appropriate party) should deploy good Problem Management techniques and discover why these 300 laptops have gone missing. Use this information to improve the asset management processes. • **COBIT**: BAI9, DSS3 • **CMMI-SVC**: WMP SP 1.OPD; CM; IRP • **ISO20K**: 4.5.4, 4.5.5, 8.2, 9.1 • **ITIL**: CSI 4.1
2. Can the current architecture accommodate the issue?	• Presumably. It seems there is some level of control and management – the current issue doesn't seem to be chronic.
3. Do we have the necessary competencies to design the required change(s)?	• The small IT team was able to create a PC asset register and collect current information. What is lacking now are the overall controls necessary to ensure equipment is properly identified, controlled, deployed and managed. • **COBIT**: BAI6, BAI7, BAI9, BAI10

Anchor	Discussion
	• **CMMI-SVC**: CM; GG 2 • **ISO20K**: 9.1, 9.2, 9.3 • **ITIL**: ST 4.2, 4.3, 4.4
V. Planning and Use of Resources	
1. What resources are required to resolve the situation (e.g. people, capital, technical...)?	• The IT Director must recognize the process improvements will require funding as well as appropriate training or even re-training. • **CMMI-SVC**: OPF; GP 2.3
2. Can the required resources be acquired?	• It shouldn't be an issue as long as the leadership recognizes the impact of the missing PCs to the overall market standing of the organization. This event is not something that should be "swept under the rug" and ignored, even though the full impact is not stated in the caselet.
3. Is the necessary data and information available, collected and managed to resolve the current situation and prevent future occurrence?	• The organization has collected the data and is beginning the investigation into a resolution. We would assume once the IT Director's concerns were answered there would be specific changes to ensure the cause is remedied and monitored.

Improvement Model Application

The scenario circumstances describe an organization that recognizes there is a need to improve their asset management practices. We don't know if there has been any business impact. We have seen steps in the IT department that truly follow the elements of PDCA and they should continue that journey. What they should add is a clearly defined policy around the management of the PCs – we have seen over and over again in industry, PCs going missing because of lax controls when it comes time to upgrade. These actions can be easily translated across the enterprise as necessary.

Solution References:

Primary Solution:

All four frameworks offer support in the solution – ISO/IEC 20000-1 provides the detail around the application of a PDCA management system, ITIL provides detail around necessary elements of asset management and components of a security policy, COBIT specifies required governance factors and CMMI-SVC provides guidance to support planning and monitoring of resource management. As a solution is developed, this organization needs to ensure the regulatory, statutory or other legal requirements are met. Lastly, even if IT "gets their asset house in order," it will make absolutely no difference if the new policies are not endorsed by top management and communicated to the user community – this is not just an IT issue! IT should take the lead, but it is an enterprise compliance issue and it should be treated as such.

CHAPTER 10:
CASELET #6 – STRATEGIC ALIGNMENT

The Board of Directors for a regional telecommunications provider presented its annual guidance (e.g., goals, strategy, funding) to the organization's management team. The primary goal for the upcoming year is to gain market share. The management team (C-level) must develop plans that will support the achievement of the Board's directives, focusing specifically on the initiatives that help the organization reach this goal. Past history has shown IT has been proactively involved (through good Business Relationship Management) in the achievement of previous annual goals. Additionally, IT is considered to be strategic in nature and leverages mature service management processes.

Recently, the Steering Committee, a new group chartered to promote communication and prioritization between the business and IT, has reviewed and accepted several requests for new projects. Reviewing their impact, metrics show a decrease in meeting stakeholder requirements, wasted resources (e.g., release re-routing), poor quality functionality from a usability view as well as a support view (e.g., higher incident rates, lack of information at the service desk and service outages) and frustrated consumers. From a user standpoint, satisfaction scores are at an all-time low.

Upon further review, the business cases for these projects that have been accepted were "bullied" through the process by the project sponsors, taking advantage of the new committee. The projects themselves haven't been bad ideas but they have not directly supported the strategic goals of the organization. In fact, most of the business cases are focused on cost-cutting (can you really argue with saving money??) rather than the Board's directive of market growth. The CIO, recognizing the lack of strategic alignment, has called a management team meeting to discuss the new business cases, the process in which they were accepted, the outcomes of their deployment and the absence of conformance to the Board of Director initiatives.

In preparation of this meeting, what improvement (process, strategy, etc...) initiatives should the CIO consider?

The Five Anchors

Anchor	Discussion
I. Strategic Alignment: IT Services to Business Objectives	
1. What are the business strategy, goals and objectives? *Are there any measures that demonstrate the achievement of the business strategy, goals and objectives?*	• This organization has been given specific guidance to gain market share and focus on initiatives that help reach this goal. Metrics show the portfolio investments are not congruent with the governing body's intent. In fact, projects are more focused on cost-cutting rather than the achievement of market growth. • **COBIT**: EDM2, APO5 • **CMMI-SVC**: STSM; GP 2.10; GP 3.2 • **ITIL**: SS 4.1, 4.2, 4.5; ST 4.6
2. What is the business issue, or activity at risk?	• The main risk is the new Steering Committee. The decisions to fund projects are focusing on cost-cutting rather than market growth. As a result, resources are being applied inappropriately to initiatives that do not support stakeholder needs. Has the Steering Committee been chartered correctly with the appropriate decision authority as well as span of control and delegation authority? • **COBIT**: Organizational Structures enabler • **CMMI-SVC**: GPs 2.3, 2.4, 2.10

Anchor	Discussion
3. Is the ownership to resolve the issue at the appropriate level of authority?	• Yes, the initiative sits with the management team.
II. Security, Compliance and Risk Issues	
1. Has there been a compromise of the information security policy?	• Unknown with the information provided.
2. What are the internal and external compliance or regulatory concerns?	• Unknown with the information provided.
3. What is the cultural appetite for risk?	• The organizational appetite for risk is presumably high (for example, the initiative of market growth). But that initiative was prescribed without any guidance to management regarding risk tolerance. In this case, the Steering Committee, which by definition is a governing body, has failed to govern and truly reduced themselves to a 'management board', which is reflected in the approval of cost-cutting initiatives. Even though they are good initiatives, they are outside the scope of the Board of Directors' guidance. The failure to separate governance from management has caused a management-based reaction resulting in wasted resources and a failure to meet the Board's directives.

Anchor	Discussion
	• **COBIT**: EDM3
	• **CMMI-SVC**: RSKM; OPF
III. Value-based Portfolio	
1. Does the current portfolio meet expectations and needs of the stakeholder?	• Obviously not. The increase of market share, although known by all, has not been achieved. Portfolio investments are focused on outcomes that are the complete opposite of the governing body's intent. • **COBIT**: APO5 • **CMMI-SVC**: STSM; GP 2.10 • **ITIL**: SS 4.2
2. What is the value of the affected business activity (VBF)?	• Unknown with the information provided.
3. Does the portfolio have the right mix of resources to deliver business benefit?	• Clearly the resources are available, but the focus is in the wrong areas as per the Board of Directors' initiatives.
IV. Design and Architecture	
1. Will the current architecture effectively resolve the issue? Is it feasible?	• This is truly a management issue rather than a technology solution. The Steering Committee is operating inappropriately and needs to refocus on the Board of Directors' initiatives.
2. Can the current architecture accommodate the issue?	• Based on past performance of IT and their ability to address previous initiatives, the assumption is yes, the architecture will handle the perceived changes.

Anchor	Discussion
3. Do we have the necessary competencies to design the required change(s)?	• Based on past performance of IT and their ability to address previous initiatives, the assumption is yes, the competencies are available and can handle the perceived changes.
V. Planning and Use of Resources	
1. What resources are required to resolve the situation (e.g. people, capital, technical...)?	• Presumed yes, but there is no direct evidence.
2. Can the required resources be acquired?	• Presumed yes, but there is no direct evidence.
3. Is the necessary data and information available, collected and managed to resolve the current situation and prevent future occurrence?	• Presumed yes, but there is no direct evidence.

Improvement Model Application

This is a classic model where the separation of governance and management has been widely misunderstood by management. In this case, management (Steering Committee) has either avoided or ignored governing body guidance (willingly or not) and so is not supporting stakeholder needs by approving initiatives that will ensure benefits.

Solution References:

Primary Solution:

The COBIT Implementation Model is a logical fit for this issue because there are a multitude of pain points and drivers that command attention to this model. These are explicit elements identified within the Implementation Model and are clearly indicated in the case. They include:

- Decrease in meeting stakeholder requirements
- Wasted resources (for example, release re-routing)
- Poor-quality functionality
- Higher incident rates
- A new business strategy/priority.

By using pain points or trigger events as the launching point for the CIO's improvement suggestions, the Board of Directors can clearly see the link between the current state and their desired goals, thus, endorsing the CIO's improvements. This is Step 1 of the Implementation Model. The CIO now has a clear path for developing the business case to launch the improvements.

Through the review of the pain points and drivers, the CIO realized management and governance experienced a disconnect in that the governing direction was ignored in the management practices (the acceptance of cost-cutting initiatives rather than growth). So, Step 2 of the Implementation Model is critical – the organizational mission, vision, goals and objectives must be clearly defined and then assimilated throughout management. The Steering Committee needs to be re-chartered to align with the clarified mission, vision, goals and objectives. The remaining steps of the model are self-explanatory.

Secondary Solution:

Having clarified the strategy in response to pain points, the organization can use specific practices from CMMI-SVC to design and plan improvements. During the execution of projects, risk management, ongoing monitoring, staff development and communication with stakeholders can be improved using PAs for managing risk and institutionalized with generic practices focussing on authority, resources, training and communication with stakeholders.

CHAPTER 11:
CASELET #7 – SECURITY, COMPLIANCE & RISK

A small, online retailer processes approximately 50,000 credit card transactions per year and is required to be Level 3 PCI compliant, which it has maintained for the last several years. The retail activities are their main line of business. In the last several months, the global industry has experienced several major security breaches which has resulted in widespread media exposure. The nefarious hacking community has achieved new heights in breaking security controls and compromising sensitive data. The company's management team has paid close attention to current events and as a result, directed a full security audit by their third-party auditor.

The results of the audit revealed multiple areas that require "immediate" attention in both PCI-compliant systems as well as non-PCI systems. The internal compliance team concurs with the recommendations but the IT organization is quite resistant. The security policy clearly states that a higher level of risk tolerance is acceptable (i.e., less stringent controls) in areas not directly related to their PCI-compliant systems. Resources are currently constrained due to:

- A backlog in Level 2 and Level 3 incidents
- Open problem tickets
- Chartered project workload
- Available funding

The CEO has authorized the IT Director to develop an improvement plan. This plan must meet the needs of all stakeholders, ensuring the recommendations are properly prioritized and addressed, as well as improving the security policy, clearly defining organizational risk tolerance and the corresponding appropriate security controls to maintain PCI compliance and overall organizational security.

The Five Anchors

Anchor	Discussion
I. Strategic Alignment: IT Services to Business Objectives	
1. What are the business strategy, goals and objectives? Are there any measures that demonstrate the achievement of the business strategy, goals and objectives?	• There is no indicator of what the business strategy is other than gaining a comfort level with their security posture. A key principle to governance is communicating the business strategy and priorities. • **COBIT**: EDM1, EDM3, EDM5 • **CMMI-SVC**: STSM; GP 2.10 • **ITIL**: SS 4.1
2. What is the business issue or activity at risk?	• Retail revenue is the primary driver for the business, so security and compliance activities should clearly focus on this. The risk of a compromise could severely damage the core business. There is no additional information regarding the vital business functions that could be at risk if a security vulnerability was compromised. • **COBIT**: APO12, APO13, DSS5 • **CMMI-SVC**: SCON; OPF • **ISO20K**: 6.6 • **ITIL**: SD 4.7
3. Is the ownership to resolve the issue at the appropriate level of authority?	• It is understood at the executive level that security risks exist and the IT Director has been assigned the task of developing an improvement plan. Although all stakeholders will be involved, the IT director might not be the appropriate owner of the plan since risk and security concerns

Anchor	Discussion
	are enterprise-wide issues and not just IT. • **COBIT**: EDM3, APO12, APO13 • **CMMI-SVC**: SCON; SM; GP 2.4 • **ISO20K**: 4.1, 6.6 • **ITIL**: SS 4.1
II. Security, Compliance and Risk Issues	
1. Has there been a compromise of the information security policy?	• The current policy is clearly insufficient. There has not been an identified breach, but the policy needs to be updated and improved. It is not known how old the current policy is, but we can assume it has not been updated recently to align with the current threat landscape. • **COBIT**: APO13 • **CMMI-SVC**: GP 2.1; SM • **ISO20K**: 6.6 • **ITIL**: SS 4.1; SD 4.7
2. What are the internal and external compliance or regulatory concerns?	• PCI compliance is the primary compliance concern for this company. It is assumed others exist, but are not identified in this caselet.
3. What is the cultural appetite for risk?	• The current security policy recognizes risk. There is a lower risk tolerance for systems within PCI scope, but no further guidance is provided. So, we can assume aggressive mitigation over PCI-associated controls. Controls for non-PCI-related activities might have less stringent controls to balance performance and conformance. • **COBIT**: EDM3, APO12

Anchor	Discussion
	• **CMMI-SVC**: RSKM; GP 2.1
III. Value-based Portfolio	
1. Does the current portfolio meet expectations and needs of the stakeholder?	• There is no mention of the services portfolio other than online retail sales.
2. What is the value of the affected business activity (VBF)?	• Since online retail sales are the core, all activities associated with this is the current assumed vital business function.
3. Does the portfolio have the right mix of resources to deliver business benefit?	• Unknown based on the information provided.
IV. Design and Architecture	
1. Will the current architecture effectively resolve the issue? Is it feasible?	• There is no information on the current architecture that suggests the ability to resolve the issue. The caselet indicates a backlog of incident and problem tickets, which could indicate there are architectural issues but this should not be assumed.
2. Can the current architecture accommodate the issue?	• There is no information on the current architecture that indicates the ability or inability to resolve the issue. The backlog of incident and problem tickets may imply architectural issues but this should not be assumed.
3. Do we have the necessary competencies to	• There is no information on staff competencies and their ability to design the necessary/required changes. With the incident and

Anchor	Discussion
design the required change(s)?	problem ticket backlog, one could assume the current architecture cannot support the necessary/required changes but there is nothing in the caselet to support that assumption.
V. Planning and Use of Resources	
1. What resources are required to resolve the situation (e.g. people, capital, technical...)?	• The IT department is resisting the effort due to resource constraints. The resources needed are being used on other activities. There is an additional concern regarding available funding for this initiative. • **COBIT**: APO7, BAI4 • **CMMI-SVC**: SM; OPF • **ISO20K**: 4.4, 6.5 • **ITIL**: SD 4.5 • **SFIA** (*www.sfia-online.org*)
2. Can the required resources be acquired?	• Since the organization used an external company to conduct the audit, they are most likely open to using external resources to assist their mitigation efforts. Before acquiring additional resources, a strong look at what is currently available is prudent. If there is no centralized portfolio, consider collecting the elements as quickly as possible to ensure there is no redundancy or overspend. • **COBIT**: EDM4, APO5 • **CMMI-SVC**: SSD; SAM • **ISO20K**: 4.4 • **ITIL**: SS 4.2; SD 4.5
3. Is the necessary data and information	• We can assume the information required is available to resolve

Anchor	Discussion
available, collected and managed to resolve the current situation and prevent future occurrence?	the current situation and prevent future occurrence.

Improvement Model Application

The COBIT Implementation Model is the best fit for this issue as COBIT has its roots in security, risk and compliance. This caselet has a clear focus on the improvement of compliance and assurance within sales transactions. The Implementation Model links COBIT practices and activities to industry standards such as PCI-DSS. The model also helps determine the most relevant controls based on the environment. These controls are then prioritized based on risk and business need. The outcome is a phased approach, which allows this organization to manage their resource constraints. The value proposition for this organization is delivering benefits while optimizing risks and resources.

Solution References:

Primary Solution:

This is a classic case of reacting to external events rather than continually monitoring and adapting to the current environment to stay abreast of risks. This organization needs to formalize a Security Management process that will:

- Apply the policy to the various scenarios to reflect organizational risk tolerance
- Define the necessary security controls for PCI activities
- Develop a formal Security Management process that integrates with Incident and Problem Management.

To accomplish these activities, the following resources provide best practice information:

- ISO/IEC 27001 for the development of the Information Security Management System (ISMS) and best practice controls
- COBIT: APO13, DSS5
- CMMI-SVC: OPD, OPF, SCON
- ISO20K: 6.6
- ITIL: SD 4.7.

Process deployment and/or improvement has no benefit unless the correct resources and capabilities are available. Ensure the portfolio accurately defines the required resources, including staff. Use SFIA to define the various roles and competencies. Using SCON practices from CMMI-SVC can help both to identify crucial assets and functions and to get the buy-in of staff to proactively protect these assets.

CHAPTER 12:
CASELET #8 – VALUE-BASED PORTFOLIO

A west coast-based technical staffing agency has experienced significant growth in the last five years and plans to expand nationally through acquisitions. However, several large customers have moved to competitors for staffing services. With the loss of these key customers, it will be difficult to meet corporate growth goals.

An investigation team was chartered to discover why customers were leaving. Their results revealed the following:

- Information provided to customers was often late, inaccurate, or not available at all
- The company primarily uses spreadsheets, even though there are systems in place to manage information
- There are multiple tools in place with little collaboration between them
- No single reporting system is used
- IT is generally viewed as a 'desktop' support team and provides little strategic contribution

All of these issues point to the fact that IT services are not providing the necessary utility and warranty and technology has not kept up with the organizational growth.

There is no designated CIO within the staffing agency but there is a technical manager, who is a direct report to the CFO, overseeing a small technical team. The IT management activities are very reactive though no one can fault any member of that team for lack of dedication or technical competency.

The CFO has directed Technical Manager to develop and recommend possible solutions which will address the current issues. The Technical Manager recognizes the immediacy for an operational solution but the entire situation, to ensure the growth of the staffing firm, requires a more tactical and strategic-based plan of action within IT. What specifically should be included in this plan?

The Five Anchors

Anchor	Discussion
I. Strategic Alignment: IT Services to Business Objectives	
1. What are the business strategy, goals and objectives? Are there any measures demonstrate the achievement of the business strategy, goals and objectives?	• Clearly, the CFO and Technical Manager need to collaborate and create a strategy that will allow IT to meet corporate objectives. That strategy must assess and define the necessary resources and capabilities to support the achievement of the business objectives. • **COBIT**: EDM1, EDM4, APO1, APO2, APO5, MEA1 • **CMMI-SVC**: SSD; WP SG 1 • **ISO20K**: 4.1, 4.5 • **ITIL**: SS 4.1, 4.2
2. What is the business issue, or activity at risk?	• The business issue is simple – this agency is losing business because the services provided by the current IT structure lack utility and warranty. The services are out of date and lack the innovation required to meet corporate goals. • **COBIT**: EDM2, APO4, APO5, BAI2 • **CMMI-SVC**: SSD • **ISO20K**: • **ITIL**: SS 4.5; SD 4.4; ST 4.6
3. Is the ownership to resolve the issue at the appropriate level of authority?	• The CFO is an 'acting head' of the IT group, current led by a Technical Manager. The question that must be asked is this: "Has the Technical Manager been clearly empowered to take ownership and resolve the

Anchor	Discussion
	situation? It is clear from the caselet that decision-making still resides with the CFO. • **COBIT**: EDM1, APO7 • **CMMI-SVC**: GP 2.4 • **ISO20K**: 4.1 • **ITIL**: SS 4.1
II. Security, Compliance and Risk Issues	
1. Has there been a compromise of the information security policy?	• Unknown with the information provided.
2. What are the internal and external compliance or regulatory concerns?	• Unknown with the information provided.
3. What is the cultural appetite for risk?	• It can be presumed there is a fairly high risk tolerance, if only due to the fact that there was high growth with no concern for aging systems and processes (a very 'start-up' mentality). Now, the reality is their high-risk tolerance has become a detriment. • **COBIT**: APO11, APO12 • **CMMI-SVC**: RSKM
III. Value-based Portfolio	
1. Does the current portfolio meet expectations and needs of the stakeholder?	• Evidently, this organization does not. It could be presumed there is no clear idea of how to define and manage the resources to meet stakeholder expectations. Not only is an operational solution needed but also a more

Anchor	Discussion
	strategic view of the requirements to meet the organizational objectives is mandatory. • **COBIT**: APO5, BAI2 • **CMMI-SVC**: SSD • **ISO20K**: 4.4, 5.2 • **ITIL**: SS 4.2
2. What is the value of the affected business activity (VBF)?	• Technical staffing is the core business activity. The fact that the organization is failing in its delivery is critical. Immediate action is required to save this organization.
3. Does the portfolio have the right mix of resources to deliver business benefit?	• It is clear from the caselet there are available and unused resources, although they might be the 'wrong' resources – both from a technology and human view. There must be a specific project to define the resources needed for service delivery and the work to achieve them. • **COBIT**: EDM4, APO5, APO7, APO10 • **CMMI-SVC**: SSD; SD SG 2 • **ISO20K**: 4.4, 6.5, 7.2 • **ITIL**: SS 4.2, SD 4.5, 4.8
IV. Design and Architecture	
1. Will the current architecture effectively resolve the issue? Is it feasible?	• Unknown with the information provided.
2. Can the current architecture	• Unknown with the information provided.

Anchor	Discussion
accommodate the issue?	
3. Do we have the necessary competencies to design the required change(s)?	• Unknown with the information provided.
V. Planning and Use of Resources	
1. What resources are required to resolve the situation (e.g. people, capital, technical...)?	• Clearly there should be a needs assessment, an overhaul of current tools, a definition of required capabilities and a clear budget to update the capabilities to meet organizational and customer demands. • **COBIT**: EDM4, APO5, APO6, APO7, BAI9, MEA1 • **CMMI-SVC**: SSD • **ISO20K**: 4.4, 4.5 (4.5.4), 5.2, 5.3, 6.4, 9.1 • **ITIL**: SS 4.2, ST 4.3, SO 6.4, 6.6 • **SFIA** (*www.sfia-online.org*)
2. Can the required resources be acquired?	• It would be logical to assume resources could be acquired as the lack of them is affecting the core business. Most importantly, this organization needs to remember that strategic plans and a clearly defined service must drive those acquisitions (perform a needs assessment).
3. Is the necessary data and information available, collected and managed to resolve the current	• The results of the investigation provide clear evidence of deficiencies. With an immediate operational solution in mind, the understanding that a more

Anchor	Discussion
situation and prevent future occurrence?	tactical and strategic solution is required will be a true benefit to this organization. Actions are not given so it is hoped the CFO accepts the need for a far-reaching solution.

Improvement Model Application

This situation demands a clear grasp of organizational need. Although all improvement models have the element of understanding the organizational vision, the CSI Approach is perhaps the clearest. The very first step of 'What is the vision?' requires the confirmation of organizational goals and objectives as well as the definition of a future state ('Where do we want to be?'). Both steps drive the development of a strategy that is clearly needed before the development of process and/or service improvements.

Solution References:

Primary Solution:

Both ITIL and COBIT give clear guidance on the definition of a strategy for the service provider as well as managing the resources and capabilities in a service portfolio. COBIT's control process of APO2 and APO5 as well as ITIL's StM and SPM processes provide the necessary information for this organization to create the policies needed to guide the IT organization, linking their actions to the achievement of business objectives.

Having established strategy and policy, CMMI-SVC practices from SSD help organizations match needs to solutions. OPF and generic practices help with organizational processes and checks to maintain good practice.

Secondary Solution:

ISO20K: The entire standard is defined around the development and management of a Service Management System (SMS). The development of a service management policy and associated plans provide necessary boundaries for the service provider and although not specifically mentioned, the governance crucial for the delivery of necessary services. Within the SMS, resources are managed and leadership is defined. Using the minimum requirements defined by ISO/IEC 20000-1 and the knowledge provided in ITIL and COBIT, this organization can effectively and efficiently create plans and actions to resolve the current deficiencies.

CHAPTER 13:
CASELET #9 – STRATEGIC CHOICE & MARKET CONDITIONS

A taxi service located in a major city within the United States has used an unusual business model and organizational structure for decades. The service is self-organized by a group of peer drivers with only loose connections to the usual large taxi companies found in cities. The drivers develop their own repeat customers; offer fixed pricing to predictable locations (such as airports and universities) to known customers; develop their own policies and processes; source their own technologies; and manage requests, demand, capacity and availability as peers. The original team leader passed away years ago, but the team is still known by his name and his business model is still followed. Some customers have been loyal for 30 years. This model developed out of the city's industrial past. Demographics that included strong unions and communities that encouraged self-reliance and independence from large enterprises.

The metropolitan area has a strong technology base and is seeing an influx of large technology companies. With this comes a change in demographics that includes hip, young populations who are strong users of ride-sharing services available through apps. Now one of these companies has established a major centre in the city and self-driving cars are adding to the growing competition from ride-sharing with drivers.

The teams of peer drivers scoffed at the ability of apps to replace their superb service and they are holding on to long-time customers. Further, they do things that ride-sharing services cannot. For example, the team offers a door-to-door service driving passengers from the city to another major city, at a more attractive price than flying. Drivers for app-based services are restricted to an area. But the competition from app-based ride sharing is eating into the team's profits and they aren't finding new, younger customers nor younger drivers to mentor and develop into team members to replace retiring members.

They need to decide as a team whether they should retire, disband, switch to ride sharing, or innovate. Most of the team wants to try a mix of their business model while adding more ride sharing – if they can figure out the agreements and live with more requirements and oversight.

The Five Anchors

Anchor	Discussion
I. Strategic Alignment: IT Services to Business Objectives	
1. What are the business strategy, goals and objectives? *Are there any measures that demonstrate the achievement of the business strategy, goals and objectives?*	• The taxi team wants to stay together and keep some of their historical mode of operation. Most recognize they will have to adapt to ride sharing and that some will retire. The goals are to keep revenue steady plus attract new customers and drivers. If they cannot see a way to do this as a team, they may disband. Measures include total team revenue, attrition of customers and drivers and acquisition of new customers. • **CMMI-SVC**: STSM; DAR; MA • **ITIL**: SS 4.1, 4.2, 4.3, 4.4
2. What is the business issue, or activity at risk?	• The survival, change, or retirement of their service. • **COBIT**: APO4, BAI5 • **CMMI-SVC**: SST; STSM
3. Is the ownership to resolve the issue at the appropriate level of authority?	• The team has made choices together in the past and they are unusual in having a self-defined structure and little governance or outside management. • **COBIT**: APO1 • **CMMI-SVC**: GG 2 • **ISO20K**: 4.1

Anchor	Discussion
II. Security, Compliance and Risk Issues	
1. Has there been a compromise of the information security policy?	• No, but team members are considering whether they can act as ride-sharing drivers while staying on the team and what policies they will have to learn and accept from the app company. • **CMMI-SVC**: GP 2.1; OPF
2. What are the internal and external compliance or regulatory concerns?	• This will depend on the solution chosen. If they form agreements with government entities to be a preferred provider, they recognize they will have to pay attention to government regulations; if they agree to cooperate with ride-sharing technology companies, they face a different raft of policies and procedures to comply with. • **COBIT**: MEA3 • **CMMI-SVC**: SSD; OPF
3. What is the cultural appetite for risk?	• They have proven to be open to risks that come with innovation in the past, often among early adopters of technologies – the first to use mobile phones in the late 1980s and mobile pay in the early part of this century. But most of the team could also retire, so individuals vary widely in their stance toward risk. Given they are self-directed peers, it is hard to discern a single appetite for risk, but they strike a balance between independence and what benefits the team. • **COBIT**: EDM3

Anchor	Discussion
	• **CMMI-SVC**: RSKM
III. Value-based Portfolio	
1. Does the current portfolio meet expectations and needs of the stakeholder?	• The team is the stakeholder for the current strategic decision and they have recognized that their offerings, operating style and customer acquisition are threatened. • **COBIT**: APO5 • **CMMI-SVC**: STSM; SSD • **ITIL**: SS 4.2
2. What is the value of the affected business activity (VBF)?	• They would be wise to make this more explicit as they decide their future. • **COBIT**: APO5 • **CMMI-SVC**: MA • **ITIL**: SS 4.2
3. Does the portfolio have the right mix of resources to deliver business benefit?	• The team believes they do have the resources to deliver business benefit, but the challenge is deciding how to change what they deliver. • **COBIT**: APO5 • **CMMI-SVC**: SSD • **ITIL**: SS 4.2
IV. Design and Architecture	
1. Will the current architecture effectively resolve the issue? Is it feasible?	• The current architecture of their service system is nearly all implicit knowledge embodied in the current drivers and passed on by mentoring to new drivers. Some members have experimented with app-based driving and believe the team can incorporate some of it into their existing architecture of processes and other resources.

Anchor	Discussion
	• **COBIT**: BAI8 • **CMMI-SVC**: SSD; DAR
2. Can the current architecture accommodate the issue?	• It can accommodate many of the components, such as cars, drivers and driving and payment processes. The team's concerns are about whether adapting apps will destroy or supplant their core business and how much overhead and oversight they may add if they seek new business. • **CMMI-SVC**: SSD
3. Do we have the necessary competencies to design the required change(s)?	• Yes. The question is whether they want to do so. • **CMMI-SVC**: GP 2.3; SSD; DAR
V. Planning and Use of Resources	
1. What resources are required to resolve the situation (e.g. people, capital, technical...)?	• The key resource after they make a decision will be negotiating the specific agreements with new customers or new services or existing companies. • **COBIT**: APO9 • **CMMI-SVC**: SSD; SD • **ISO20K**: 6.1 • **ITIL**: SD 4.3
2. Can the required resources be acquired?	• Yes, but a challenge for this team is that they are fundamentally self-directed and negotiations will require empowering someone to negotiate for them. They would be wise to charter themselves and choose roles during this period. • **COBIT**: APO1 • **CMMI-SVC**: GG 2

Anchor	Discussion
	• **ISO20K**: 4.1
3. Is the necessary data and information available, collected and managed to resolve the current situation and prevent future occurrence?	• Yes. Although some of their understanding of trends and market forces are anecdotal, they have measurable and shared information on rides, revenue and the like that give them facts. • **COBIT**: Information Enabler • **CMMI-SVC**: STSM; MA

Improvement Model Application

This case is fundamentally about using market data and decision processes to redesign the service system the taxi team uses. CMMI-SVC has process areas to do each of these: collect and analyse data about a portfolio, analyse and resolve decisions (whether strategic, technical, or tactical) and design or redesign the portfolio and the service system. The use of STSM and DAR may then be obvious. What may be less obvious is SSD can also be powerful during such a decision, because the practices in SSD are used to reason about a service system, whether the goal is to build a new one or to change it. Some of the practices allow service professionals to experiment with the feasibility of particular solutions and to anticipate how interfaces would work, which would be a boon to the taxi team as they decide their future. These interfaces could be among people, organizations and processes – not just technical components. The crucial interfaces with the ride-sharing company can be considered. The challenge for the taxi company is that they have deep implicit – even unconscious – knowledge about their work. This decision would benefit from making their knowledge visible and tangible while they consider their options. Once they decide, they could use SST to guide their actions whether they change or retire their service system.

Solution References:

Primary Solution:

CMMI for Services has the practices to help the taxi team analyse data, decide which strategy is best and then design or transition their service system to execute the chosen strategy. Although people often think of process improvement and compliance when they think of CMMI, note that this application is about transforming strategy in a very small service setting that is not IT.

Secondary Solution:

COBIT, the ISO/IEC 20000 family of standards and ITIL all have practices that are explicit in their application which would benefit this company. The adopt and adapt team would benefit discovering the implicit practices. With a bit of creativity, these frameworks, although based in IT, can be applied to everyday business practices.

CHAPTER 14:
CASELET #10 – PLAN & USE RESOURCES

A metropolitan urgent care organization has 20 facilities located in a major city within the United States and has plans to open an additional 10 facilities in the surrounding suburbs. This organization is a result of two mergers within the last three years. Work to consolidate and standardize the technology architecture has been slow due to financial constraints. There is a central data centre that provides shared services for the entire enterprise but support services are inconsistent across all facilities.

Dedicated onsite IT staff teams support between three to five facilities based on patient volumes. IT employee turnover has been very high due to poor salaries, frustration with inconsistent infrastructure and lack of career opportunities. Approximately 30% of the IT workforce are contractors.

Additionally, this organization must keep within federal mandates. A major project is underway to roll out an Electronic Medical Records (EMR) system. The project is halfway through a 15-month plan. Furthermore, ten new facilities are scheduled to open in the next six months.

The IT director is overwhelmed with the complexity of the EMR rollout, the architecture updates as well as continuing federal requirements. As a result, he has hired an external expert to help the IT organization design a plan that will address the current difficulties. You are the external expert. What do you recommend?

The Five Anchors

Anchor	Discussion
I. Strategic Alignment: IT Services to Business Objectives	
1. What are the business strategy, goals and objectives? Are there any measures that demonstrate the achievement of the business strategy, goals and objectives?	• The strategy of the organization is clear – growth via mergers, address federal mandates and consolidate/standardize the technological architecture.

2. What is the business issue, or activity at risk?	• The EMR rollout (federally mandated) is at risk due to the current infrastructure and the planned updates.
	  • **COBIT**: EDM2, EDM4, APO3, MEA3
	  • **CMMI-SVC**: SST

3. Is the ownership to resolve the issue at the appropriate level of authority?	• The IT director is the owner of the issues but is at a loss of how to manage the situation. Even though he lacks the necessary knowledge and skill for this, he obviously has the authority to hire an expert.
	  • **COBIT**: APO7
	  • **CMMI-SVC**: GP 2.4
	  • **ISO20K**: 4.1

II. Security, Compliance and Risk Issues	
1. Has there been a compromise of the information security policy?	• Unknown with the information provided.

Anchor	Discussion
2. What are the internal and external compliance or regulatory concerns?	• There is a federal mandate to deploy a system to support EMR. The mandated time to complete the project is fast approaching (and may be hindered by current infrastructure issues as well as the continued expansion of the urgent care facilities). • **COBIT**: MEA3 • **CMMI-SVC**: SST; WP SG 1
3. What is the cultural appetite for risk?	• It seems to be quite high – the expansion continues, whereas the supporting structures and the completion of federally mandated initiatives lag behind. • **COBIT**: EDM3, APO3 • **CMMI-SVC**: RSKM
III. Value-based Portfolio	
1. Does the current portfolio meet expectations and needs of the stakeholder?	• No. Staff supporting the urgent care centers are overworked and under supported. There is a high turnover and 30 percent of the current staff are contractors. Technology resources are lacking due to budgets and may be aging rapidly. There is no consistent architecture that causes compatibility issues. It is unclear from the caselet if it is even known exactly what is needed to support the improvement efforts, continued expansion and the EMR project. • **COBIT**: EDM5, APO3, APO5 • **CMMI-SVC**: SSD; SST; SD • **ITIL**: SS 4.1, 4.2

Anchor	Discussion
2. What is the value of the affected business activity (VBF)?	• If only including the federally mandated EMR project in the value calculation, the entire organization is at risk. The specific implications of non-compliance are not documented in the caselet, but logic states this organization would be a risk for continued operation. The level of stress felt by the IT Director is valid. • **COBIT**: EDM2 • **CMMI-SVC**: SCON • **ITIL**: SD 4.4, 4.6
3. Does the portfolio have the right mix of resources to deliver business benefit?	• Yes and no. Obviously, the infrastructure and associated technology is not necessarily deficient (it is functional!), but it lacks consistency. A refresh in design and components (which is underway) is required. Staff are questionable – they are underpaid and over-utilized – but again, systems and locations are functioning. A complete review of the exact services to be delivered along with clear business-based requirements (including the federally mandated requirements) needs to be developed and an overall strategy and funding to achieve those requirements is mandatory. • **COBIT**: APO5 • **CMMI-SVC**: SSD; PPQA; OPF • **ISO20K**:4.5 • **ITIL**: SS 4.2

Anchor	Discussion
IV. Design and Architecture	
1. Will the current architecture effectively resolve the issue? Is it feasible?	• No. The caselet clearly states the original merger has triggered a standardization and consolidation project, but it has been hampered by a lack of funds. With the many concurrent initiatives, there needs to be a definite prioritization of the projects (Steering Committee?) and once planned, definitively funded. • **COBIT**: APO3, BAI1 • **CMMI-SVC**: GPs 2.3, 2.9, 2.10, 3.2
2. Can the current architecture accommodate the issue?	• The assumption is yes as the efforts are about consolidating and standardizing rather than a complete redesign. There is no mention that the infrastructure is 'lacking'.
3. Do we have the necessary competencies to design the required change(s)?	• Unknown with the information provided. The only evidence of a lack of competency is the hiring of the consultant, which perhaps shows appropriate competency by the IT Director. • **COBIT**: APO7 • **CMMI-SVC**: SAM • **ISO20K**: 4.4 • **SFIA** (*www.sfia-online.org*)
V. Planning and Use of Resources	
1. What resources are required to resolve the situation (e.g.	• The consultant is a good place to start – hopefully the findings and recommendations are supported. Overall, the resources required

Anchor	Discussion
people, capital, technical...)?	may not be readily available or current resources need to be reassigned to meet needs. But, more than chasing resources, there should be a review of what is needed that gives rise to an appropriate plan to procure those resources. • **COBIT**: EDM4, APO7, APO10 • **CMMI-SVC**: SSD; GP 2.3
2. Can the required resources be acquired?	• This is unknown from the caselet. The organization continues to expand yet funding isn't available to increase the foundational systems, supporting infrastructure and staff. • **COBIT**: EDM4, APO7, APO10 • **CMMI-SVC**: SSD; GP 2.3
3. Is the necessary data and information available, collected and managed to resolve the current situation and prevent future occurrence?	• Unknown with the information provided.

Improvement Model Application

This organization requires a clearly defined and prioritized path that is in line with the business goals and objectives. The Goals Cascade from COBIT would be an outstanding place to start. The cascading of goals ensures proper alignment between 1) Stakeholder Needs, 2) Enterprise Goals, 3) IT Related Goals and 4) Enabler Goals. Enablers include all the factors required to ensure proper governance and management of enterprise IT. This solution fits well with the COBIT Implementation Model, which focuses on the quick wins and long-term solutions that use these enablers to ensure a holistic approach to improvement. Further information about these enablers can be found in *Chapter 2*.

Solution References:

Primary Solution:

This situation requires more than just process improvement. Using the COBIT Implementation Model with the COBIT Goals Cascade not only allows for an iterative approach to improvement but also helps create and adopt controls necessary for this organization to maintain compliance with the various industry-related requirements while ensuring alignment with stakeholder needs and enterprise goals. By using this approach, the IT Director can confirm a holistic approach to the required improvements within the following enablers:

- **Principles, Policies and Frameworks** – determining appropriate policy modifications based on the organizational principles and requirements arising from the EMR adoption.
- **Processes** – selecting processes that are most critical to meet the aggressive growth needs of the business as well as assisting in the management of critical resources.
- **Organizational Structures** – defining key levels of authorities, delegation of responsibilities and escalation procedures to support the business outcomes.
- **Culture, Ethics and Behaviours** – understanding, communicating and managing stakeholder needs and expectations.
- **Information** – as a key resource in the success of the EMR system, information can be classified and managed in a manner that allows architectural decisions to be prioritized.
- **Services, Infrastructure and Applications** – warranting the infrastructure and applications supporting the needs of the business, but linking these to services that are critical to the success of the initiative.
- **People, Skills and Competencies** – allowing the organization to understand current and future needs regarding not only staff capacity but also linking them to the skills and competencies required inside the organization.

The COBIT Implementation Model does not focus strictly on processes as many other models do. By linking stakeholder needs to enabler goals, a much more holistic view of improvement is offered. This approach is best suited to the caselet due to the wide array of issues facing the urgent care organization.

Content from CMMI-SVC aligns well with these enablers, with the use of generic practices being particularly powerful. Both these enablers and the GPs from CMMI-SVC can be used to get the right system designed – whether the system is an enterprise architecture of processes, or a mix of process, people and technology. Both COBIT and CMMI-SVC have content to encourage planning, monitoring and ongoing audit.

Secondary Solution:

ITIL: One of the key principles in the *ITIL Service Design* volume is the Five Aspects of Service Design. These aspects 'force' the architect/designer to think beyond the technological solution. As a reminder, the Five Aspects include:

- Service solution
- Management information systems and tools
- Technology and management architectures
- Processes
- Measures and metrics.

These five aspects demand a broad view of the solution but it is still a technical view. One must remember the business need as well as organizational factors that must be met with the new or changed service. The enablers from COBIT as well as the generic practices within CMMI-SVC provides the architect a true view of both the technical management requirements but also the business requirements.

APPENDIX A: THE MAP

Using the domains and processes within COBIT, we have created a mapping between ISO/IEC 20000-1:2011, ITIL 2011 and CMMI-SVC. Before jumping in and exploring the mapping, a few disclaimers are necessary:

- Processes in COBIT are not discrete when compared to ISO/IEC 20000-1, ITIL and CMMI-SVC – you may very well "see" alternate relationships.
- The numbers in the ITIL, ISO/IEC 20000-1:2011 and CMMI-SVC columns are based on section numbering within the source documents. Those numbers are reproduced in Tables 1, 2 3 and 4 in Chapter 2.
- Relationships are based on process and sub-process activity descriptions in COBIT, where it is not uncommon to see activities from multiple references in ITIL, ISO/IEC 20000-1 and CMMI-SVC.
- For CMMI-SVC, we have added only PAs up to level 3 and left out PAs that are at levels 4 or 5. Processes that have been noted in parenthesis are minor relationships.
- Where only the ITIL volume name is provided, the specific COBIT activity is assumed or underpins the entire ITIL phase.
- Supporting frameworks, standards or methodologies are listed in bold and red.

Legend for acronyms:

Acronym	Full Name
7S	7-step Improvement Process (CSI)
AcM	Access Management (SO)
AM	Availability Management (SD)
APO	Align, Plan and Organize
AppM	*Application Management (SO)**
BAI	Build, Acquire and Implement
BRM	Business Relationship Management (SS)
CapM	Capacity Management (SD)
CAR	Causal Analysis & Resolution
ChE	Change Evaluation (ST)
ChM	Change Management (ST)
CSI	**Continual Service Improvement****
CAM	Capacity & Availability Management
CM	Configuration Management
DAR	Decision Analysis & Resolution
DC	Design Coordination (SD)
DM	Demand Management (SS)
DSS	Deliver, Service and Support
EDM	Evaluate, Direct and Monitor
EM	Event Management (SO)
FM	Financial Management for IT Services (SS)
IM	Incident Management (SO)
IRP	Incident Resolution & Prevention
ISM	Information Security Management (SD)
ITOM	*IT Operations Management (SO)**
ITSCM	IT Service Continuity Management (SD)
IWM	Integrated Work Management
KM	Knowledge Management (ST)
MA	Measurement & Analysis
MEA	Monitor, Evaluate and Assess
OPD	Organizational Process Definition
OPF	Organizational Process Focus
OPM	Organizational Performance Management
OPP	Organizational Process Performance
OT	Organizational Training
PM	Problem Management (SO)
PPQA	Process & Product Quality Assurance
QWM	Quantitative Work Management

Acronym	Full Name
RDM	Release and Deployment Management (ST)
REQM	Requirements Management
RF	Request Fulfillment (SO)
RSKM	Risk Management
SACM	Service Asset and Configuration Management (ST)
SAM	Supplier Agreement Management
ScatM	Service Catalogue Management (SD)
SCON	Service Continuity
SD	Service Delivery (CMMI-SVC)
SD	**Service Design****
	Service Desk (SO)*
SLM	Service Level Management (SD)
SO	**Service Operation****
SPM	Service Portfolio Management (SS)
SS	**Service Strategy****
SSD	Service System Development
SST	Service System Transition
ST	**Service Transition****
STSM	Strategic Service Management
StM	Strategy Management for IT Services (SS)
SuppM	Supplier Management (SD)
SVT	Service Validation and Testing (ST)
TM	*Technical Management (SO)**
TPS	Transition Planning and Support (ST)
WMC	Work Monitoring & Control
WP	Work Planning

Notes: Service Desk will not be abbreviated owing to possible confusion with the Service Design volume and Service Delivery PA.

ITIL processes and functions include the source volume.

*ITIL Function   **The ITIL volume

Evaluate, Direct & Monitor (EDM)	ITIL	ISO/IEC20000-1:2011	CMMI-SVC
01 Ensure Governance Framework Setting & Maintenance (ISO/IEC 38500)			
.01 Evaluate the Governance System	SS 5.1 (4.1, 4.2); CSI 3.10	4.1	GP 2.4, GP 2.7
.02 Direct the Governance System	SS 5.1 (4.1)	4.1	GG 2; GG 3
.03 Monitor the Governance System	SS 5.1 (4.1)	4.1, 4.5	GPs 2.7, 2.10, 3.2; MA; WMC
02 Ensure Benefits Delivery			
.01 Evaluate Value Optimization	SS 3.2.3, 4.1, 4.2, 4.5	4.1, 4.2, 7.1, 7.2	GP 3.2; SSD SP 1.1,
.02 Direct Value Optimization	SS 3.2.3, 4.2, 4.5	4.1, 7.1	GG2; GG3; STSM SP 1.1
.03 Monitor Value Optimization	SS 4.1, 4.2; SD 4.3, CSI	4.1, 4.5.4, 6.2	GP 3.2; MA SP 2.4; WMC
03 Ensure Risk Optimization (ISO/IEC 31000)			
.01 Evaluate risk management	SS 4.2, 5.6.5, D.3, E	4.1.1	OPF SG 1
.02 Direct risk management	SS 4.2; SD 4.3, 4.6, 4.7	4.5.5.2	OPF SG 3; RSKM; GP 2.1
.03 Monitor risk management	SS 4.2	4.5.3	GP 2.7, WMC
04 Ensure Resource Optimization (SFIA)			
.01 Evaluate resource management	SS 5.1, 5.2, 6.10 (4.1, 4.2)	4.1, 4.4	CAM SP 1.3, SG 3
.02 Direct resource management	SS 6.10 (4.2)	4.1, 4.4	CAM SG 1; WP SP 2.4
.03 Monitor resource management	SS 6.10 (4.2)	4.1, 4.4	CAM SG 2; SD SP 3.2; GP 2.3
05 Ensure Stakeholder Transparency			
.01 Evaluate Stakeholder reporting requirements	CSI 5.7 (SS 4.5; SD 6.3)	4.1, 6.2	GP 2.7; MA SP 2.4
.02 Direct stakeholder communication & reporting	ST 5.1 (SS 4.5; SD 6.3)	4.1, 6.1, 6.2, 7.1	IWM SG 2; WP SP 2.6
.03 Monitor stakeholder communication	SS 4.5; SD 6.3 (ST 5.1)	4.1, 6.1, 6.2, 7.1	WMC SP 1.5; GP 2.7

Appendix A: The Map

Align, Plan & Organize (APO)	ITIL	ISO/IEC20000-1:2011	CMMI-SVC
01 Manage the IT Management Framework			
.01 Define the organizational structure	(SS 4.1)	4.1	GP 2.4
.02 Establish roles and responsibilities	(SS 4.1)	4.1, 4.4	GP 2.4
.03 Maintain the enablers of the management system	(SS 4.1)	4.1	GP 2.7
.04 Communicate management objectives and direction	(SS 4.1)	4.1	GP 3.2
.05 Optimize the placement of the IT function	(SS 4.1)	4.1	GP 3.2
.06 Define information (data) and system ownership	(SS 4.1)	4.1, 4.3	SD SPs 2.1, 2.2; SSD SPs 2.1, 2.2, 2.3
.07 Manage continual improvement of processes	(SS 4.1)	4.1, 4.5	OPF SP 1.3, SP 2.1
.08 Maintain compliance with policies and procedures	All	4.1	GP 2.9; PPQA
02 Manage Strategy			
.01 Understand enterprise direction	SS 4.1 (4.2, 4.5)	(4.1, 4.5)	STSM
.02 Assess the current environment, capabilities and performance	SS 4.1 (4.2, 4.5)	(4.1, 4.5)	STSM SP 1.1
.03 Define the target IT capabilities	SS 4.1 (4.2, 4.5)	(4.1, 4.5)	STSM SP 1.1
.04 Conduct a gap analysis	SS 4.1 (4.2, 4.5)	(4.1, 4.5)	STSM SP 1.2
.05 Define the strategic plan and road map	SS 4.1 (4.2, 4.5)	(4.1, 4.5)	STSM SP 1.2
.06 Communicate the IT strategy and direction	SS 4.1 (4.2, 4.5)	4.1	STSM GP 2.10
03 Manage Enterprise Architecture			
.01 Develop the enterprise architecture vision	SO 6.4; (SS, SD)	(4.0, 5.0)	OPD; SSD SG 1, SG 2
.02 Define reference architecture	SO 6.4; (SS, SD)	(4.0, 5.0)	OPD; SSD
.03 Select opportunities and solutions	SS 4.1, 4.2; CSI (SO 6.4)	(4.0, 5.0)	SSD SG 2
.04 Define architecture implementation	SO 6.4; (SS, SD)	(4.0, 5.0)	SSD SG 2; STSM SG 2
.05 Provide enterprise architecture services	SO 6.4; (SS, SD)	(4.0, 5.0) ·	SD

125

Align, Plan & Organize (APO)	ITIL	ISO/IEC20000-1:2011	CMMI-SVC
04 Manage Innovation			
.01 Create an environment conducive to innovation	(SS, SD, ST goal)		OPF SG 1
.02 Maintain an understanding of the enterprise environment	SS 4.5; SD 6.3		OPF SG 1
.03 Monitor and scan the technology environment	SD 4.5 (SS 4.2)	6.5	STSM SP 1.1
.04 Assess the potential of emerging technologies and innovation ideas	SD 4.5; ST 4.2	6.5	STSM SP 1.1; OPF SP 1.2
.05 Recommend appropriate further initiatives	SD 4.5; ST 4.2	6.5	OPF SP 1.3
.06 Monitor the implementation and use of innovation	(SS 4.2)		OPF SG 3
05 Manage Portfolio			
.01 Establish the target investment mix	SS 4.2 (4.3, 4.4)	(4.0, 5.0, 6.4)	STSM; OPF SG 1
.02 Determined the availability and sources of funds	SS 4.2 (4.3)	(4.0, 5.0, 6.4)	OPF GP 2.3
.03 Evaluate and select programs to fund	SS 4.2 (4.3, 4.4)	(4.0, 5.0, 6.4)	STSM SG 1; OPF SP 1.3
.04 Monitor, optimize and report on investment portfolio performance	SS 4.2 (SS 4.3; CSI)	(4.0, 5.0, 6.4)	MA; OPF SG 3
.05 Maintain portfolios	SS 4.2 (4.3)	(4.0, 5.0, 6.4)	STSM; OPF
.06 Manage benefits achievement	SS 4.2 (4.3)	(4.0, 5.0, 6.4)	OPF SG 3; MA
06 Manage Budget & Costs			
.01 Manage finance and accounting	SS 4.3	6.4	WMC SP 1.1
.02 Prioritize resource allocation	SS 4.2, 4.3	6.4	GP 2.3
.03 Create and maintain budgets	SS 4.3 (4.1)	6.4	WP SP 2.1
.04 Model and allocate costs	SS 4.3	6.4	WP SP 1.5
.05 Manage costs	SS 4.3	6.4	WMC SP1.1, SG 2
07 Manage Human Resources			
.01 Maintain adequate and appropriate staffing	SD 4.5; SO 6.3-6.6	4.4, 6.5	CAM; WP SP 2.4
.02 Identify key IT personnel	ST 4.7 (SS 4.2)	4.4	SD SG 2; SSD SG 2; WP SP 2.4
.03 Maintain the skills and competencies of personnel	ST 4.7, 6.6	4.4	SD SP 2.2; GP 2.5; WP SP 2.5
.04 Evaluate employee job performance	(ST 6.6)	4.4	SD SP 3.2; WMC SG 1
.05 Plan and track the usage of IT and business human resources	SS 4.2		CAM; WMC SG 1
.06 Manage contract staff	SD 4.8; SO 6.4-6.6	7.2	SD SP 3.2; CAM SP 2.1

Align, Plan & Organize (APO)	ITIL	ISO/IEC20000-1:2011	CMMI-SVC
08 Manage Relationships			
.01 Understand business expectations	SS 4.5 (4.4; SD 4.3)	7.1	SSD SG 1
.02 Identify opportunities, risk and constraints for IT to enhance the business	SS 4.5 (SD 4.5)	6.5, 7.1	STSM SG 1; REQM SP 1.3; WMC SP 1.6
.03 Manage the business relationship	SS 4.5; SD 4.3	6.1, 7.1	SD SP 1.1; REQM SG1; GP 2.7
.04 Coordinate and communicate	SD 4.3 (SS 4.5)	6.1 (7.1)	SD SG 1, SG 3; GP 2.7
.05 Provide input to the continual improvement of services	SS 4.5; SD 4.3; CSI	6.1, 7.1	STSM SP 1.1, GP 3.2
09 Manage Service Agreements			
.01 Identify IT services	SD 4.2, 4.3 (SS 4.2, 4.4)	6.1	STSM SG 2
.02 Catalogue IT-enabled services	SD 4.2 (SS 4.2)	6.1	STSM SG 2
.03 Define and prepare service agreements	SD 4.3, 4.8 (SS 4.2)	6.1, 7.2	SD SG 1
.04 Monitor and report service levels	SD 4.3 (SD 4.5; SO, CSI)	6.1, 6.2	CAM SG 2; SD SG 3
.05 Review service agreements and contracts	SD 4.3, 4.8	6.1, 7.2	SD SG 1; GP 2.8
10 Manage Suppliers			
.01 Identify and evaluate supplier relationships and contracts	SD 4.8 (SS 4.2)	7.2	SAM SG 2; SD SG 1; (GP 2.8)
.02 Select suppliers	SD 4.8	7.2	SAM SP1.2
.03 Manage supplier relationships & contracts	SD 4.8	4.2, 6.1, 7.2	SAM SG 2
.04 Manage supplier risk	SD 4.8	4.2, 7.2	SAM SG 2; GP 2.8
.05 Monitor supplier performance and compliance	SD 4.8, 4.3	4.2, 7.2	SAM SG 2
11 Manage Quality [ISO 9001]			
.01 Establish a quality management system (QMS)	CSI A.2 (SS 4.5; CSI)	(4.0)	OPD
.02 Define and manage quality standards practices and procedures	Implied CSI	(4.0)	OPD; OPF
.03 Focus quality management on customers	Implied CSI	(4.0)	SD SG 1; OPF SP 1.1; GP 2.7
.04 Perform quality monitoring, control and reviews	Implied CSI	(4.0)	GPs 2.8, 2.9, 2.10
.05 Integrate a quality management into solutions for development and service delivery	Implied CSI	(4.0)	PPQA; SD SG 2; GP 2.9
.06 Maintain continuous improvement	Implied CSI	4.5.5	OPF; GP3.2

Align, Plan & Organize (APO)	ITIL	ISO/IEC20000-1:2011	CMMI-SVC
12 Manage Risk [ISO/IEC 31000]			
.01 Collect data	SD 4.4, 4.6, 4.7, M, N.3; ST 4.2, 4.6	4.1, 4.5, 5.0, 6.3, 6.6, 9.2	SD SG 3; RSKM SG 2
.02 Analyze risk	SD 4.4, 4.6, 4.7, M, N.3; ST 4.2, 4.6	4.1, 4.5, 5.0, 6.3, 6.6, 9.2	RSKM SG 2
.03 Maintain a risk profile	Lifecycle activities	4.1, 4.5, 5.0, 6.3, 6.6, 9.2	RSKM SG 2; GP 2.6
.04 Articulate risk	ST 4.6	4.1, 4.5, 5.0, 6.3, 6.6, 9.2	RSKM SG2; SD SP 2.2; GP 2.10
.05 Define a risk management action portfolio	Lifecycle activities	4.1, 4.5, 5.0, 6.3, 6.6, 9.2	RSKM SPs 2.2, 3.2; (GP 2.6)
.06 Respond to risk	Lifecycle activities	4.1, 4.5, 5.0, 6.3, 6.6, 9.2	RSKM SG3
13 Manage Security [ISO/IEC 27000]			
.01 Establish and maintain an ISMS	SD 4.7	6.6	SM SPs 1.2, 1.5
.02 Define and manage an information security risk treatment plan	SD 4.7	6.6	SM SPs 1.2, 1.3, 1.4
.03 Monitor and review the ISMS	SD 4.7	6.6	SM SP 2.2

Build, Acquire & Implement (BAI)	ITIL	ISO/IEC20000-1:2011	CMMI-SVC
01 Manage Programs & Projects (PMI®; PRINCE2®; P3O®; Six Sigma)			
.01 Maintain a standard approach for program and project management	(SS 4.2, 4.5, 6.7, D.10; CSI 4.1)	(4.5, 5.0)	OPD SP1.1
.02 Initiate a program	(SS 4.2, 4.5, 6.7, D.10; CSI 4.1)	(4.5, 5.0)	SD SG 1; IWM SG 1
.03 Manage stakeholder engagement	(SS 4.2, 4.5, 6.7, D.10; CSI 4.1)	(4.5, 5.0)	SD GP 2.7; IWM SG 2
.04 Develop and maintain the program	(SS 4.2, 4.5, 6.7, D.10; CSI 4.1)	(4.5, 5.0)	SD; IWM
.05 Launch and execute the program	(SS 4.2, 4.5, 6.7, D.10; CSI 4.1)	(4.5, 5.0)	SD; WP
.06 Monitor, control and report on the program outcomes	(SS 4.2, 4.5, 6.7, D.10; CSI 4.1)	(4.5, 5.0)	SD SG 3; IWM SP 1.5, SG 2; GPs 2.8, 2.10; (MA)
.07 Start up and initiate projects within a program	(SS 4.2, 4.5, 6.7, D.10; CSI 4.1)	(4.5, 5.0)	SD SG 1, IWM SG 1
.08 Plan projects	(SS 4.2, 4.5, 6.7, D.10; CSI 4.1)	(4.5, 5.0)	SD SG 1; WP
.09 Manage program and project quality	(SS 4.2, 4.5, 6.7, D.10; CSI 4.1)	(4.5, 5.0)	SD; IWM SG 2; PPQA
.10 Manage program and project risk	(SS 4.2, 4.5, 6.7, D.10; CSI 4.1)	(4.5, 5.0)	SD; RSKM
.11 Monitor and control projects	(SS 4.2, 4.5, 6.7, D.10; CSI 4.1)	(4.5, 5.0)	WMC; SD; GP 2.8
.12 Manage project resources and work packages	(SS 4.2, 4.5, 6.7, D.10; CSI 4.1)	(4.5, 5.0)	WMC; IWM; GP2.3
.13 Close a project or iteration	(SS 4.2, 4.5, 6.7, D.10; CSI 4.1)	(4.5, 5.0)	SST SG 2
.14 Close a program	(SS 4.2, 4.5, 6.7, D.10; CSI 4.1)	(4.5, 5.0)	SST SG 2
02 Manage Requirements Definition			
.01 Define and maintain business functional and technical requirements	SD 3.4, 3.5, 4.3, 5.1; (SS 4.5)	5.2	SSD SG 1; SD SG 3; REQM
.02 Perform a feasibility study and formulate alternative solutions	SD 3.8.1	(5.2)	SSD SP 2.1
.03 Manage requirements risks	(SD)	5.2	REQM; RSKM SG2
.04 Obtain approval of requirements and solutions	SD 4.3	5.2	SSD SG 3

Build, Acquire & Implement (BAI)	ITL	ISO/IEC20000-1:2011	CMMI-SVC
03 Manage Solutions Identification & Build			
.01 Design high-level solutions	SD 4.1, 4.4, 4.5, 4.6; SO 6.4, 6.5, 6.6	5.3	SSD SP 2.2
.02 Design detailed solution components	SD 4.1, 4.4, 4.5, 4.6; SO 6.4, 6.5, 6.6	5.3	SSD SP 2.2
.03 Develop solution components	SD 4.4; SO 6.4, 6.5, 6.6	5.3	SSD SP 2.4
.04 Procure solution components	SS 4.3, SD 4.4, 4.8; SO 6.4, 6.5, 6.6	5.3	SAM; SSD SPs 2.4, 2.5
.05 Build solutions	ST 4.1, 4.4; SO 6.4, 6.5, 6.6	5.3	SSD SPs 2.4, 2.5
.06 Perform quality assurance	ST 4.4, 4.5, 4.6; SO 6.4, 6.5, 6.6	5.3	SSD SG 3; GP 2.9; PPQA
.07 Prepare for solution testing	ST 4.5 (4.4); SO 6.4, 6.5, 6.6	5.3	SSD SP 3.1
.08 Execute solution testing	ST 4.5 (4.4); SO 6.4, 6.5, 6.6	5.3	SSD SPs 3.3, 3.4
.09 Manage changes to requirements	ST 4.2 (SD 6.3; SS 4.5); SO 6.4, 6.5, 6.6	5.3	SSD SG 1; REQM
.10 Maintain solutions	ST 4.2, 4.3, 4.4; SO 6.4, 6.5, 6.6	5.3	SD SP 3.2; SSD SP 2.1
.11 Define IT services and maintain the service portfolio	SS 4.2; SD 4.2, 4.3; ST 4.2; SO 6.4, 6.5, 6.6	5.3	STSM SG 2
04 Manage Availability & Capacity			
.01 Assess current availability, performance and capacity and create a baseline	SD 4.4, 4.5	6.3, 6.4	CAM SG 1
.02 Assess business impact	SD 4.4, 4.5 (4.3, 4.6); ST 4.2	6.3, 6.4, 9.2	CAM SG 1
.03 Plan for new or changed service requirements	SD 4.4, 4.5; ST 4.2; CSI	6.3, 6.4	SSD SG 1; REQM; SD SG 3
.04 Monitor and review availability and capacity	SD 4.4, 4.5	6.3, 6.4	CAM SG 2
.05 Investigate and address availability , performance and capacity issues	SD 4.4, 4.5; SO 4.4	6.3, 6.4, 8.2	CAM SG 2
05 Manage Organizational Change Enablement			
.01 Establish the desire to change	ST 4.2, 5.2, C.11 (4.4)	4.1, 5.3	STSM; OPF
.02 Form an effective implementation team	ST 4.2, 5.2, C.11 (4.4)		OPF SG2; IWM SP 1.6; GPs 2.3, 2.4
.03 Communicate desired vision	ST 4.2, 5.2, C.11 (4.4)	4.1	STSM SG 1; OPF; GP 2.10
.04 Empower role players and identify short-term wins	ST 4.2, 5.2, C.11 (4.4)		OPF SP 1.1; GP 2.4, (STSM)
.05 Enable operation and use	ST 4.2, 5.2, C.11 (4.4)	5.3	SD SG 2, OPD
.06 Embed new approaches	ST 4.2, 4.7, 5.2, C.11 (4.4)		SSD; SD; OPD
.07 Sustain changes	ST 4.2, 4.7, 5.2, C.11 (4.4)		SSD; SD; STSM SG 2; OPD

Build, Acquire & Implement (BAI)	ITIL	ISO/IEC20000-1:2011	CMMI-SVC
06 Manage Changes			
.01 Evaluate, prioritize and authorize change requests	ST 4.2	9.2	SD SG 3
.02 Manage emergency changes	ST 4.2	9.2	SD SG 3
.03 Track and report change status	ST 4.2	9.2	SD SG 3; GP 2.10; GP 2.7
.04 Close and document the changes	ST 4.2	9.2	SD SG 3; GPs 2.2, (2.6)
07 Manage Change Acceptance & Transitioning			
.01 Establish an implementation plan	ST 3.1, 4.4, 4.5; SO 4.4, 4.5, 4.6	9.3	SST SP 1.2; SSD SG 2; SD SG 2
.02 Plan business process, system and data conversion	ST 4.4; SO 4.4, 4.5, 4.6	9.3	SST SG 1
.03 Plan acceptance test	SD 3.7; ST 4.4; SO 4.4, 4.5, 4.6	5.4, 9.3	SST SG 1
.04 Establish a test environment	ST 4.4, 4.5; SO 4.4, 4.5, 4.6	5.4, 9.3	SSD SG 3; SST; (GP 2.3)
.05 Perform acceptance tests	ST 4.4, 4.5; SO 4.4, 4.5, 4.6	5.4, 9.3	SSD SG 3; SST SG 1
.06 Promote to production and manage releases	ST 4.4; SO 4.4, 4.5, 4.6	9.3	SST SP 1.3, SG2; GPs 2.7, 2.8
.07 Provide early production support	ST 4.4; SO 4.4, 4.5, 4.6	9.3	SST SG1; SD SG 2; SG 3
.08 Perform a post-implementation review	ST 4.2, 4.4; SO 4.4, 4.5, 4.6	9.2	SST SP 2.2
08 Manage Knowledge			
.01 Nurture and facilitate a knowledge-sharing culture	ST 4.7, 7.1	4.3	OPF; OT; GP 2.5; WP SP 2.5
.02 Identify and classify sources of information	ST 4.7, 7.1	4.3	GP 2.3; (CM SG 1)
.03 Organize and contextualize information into knowledge	ST 4.7, 7.1	4.3	
.04 Use and share knowledge	ST 4.7, 7.1 (4.4)	4.3	SD; GPs 2.5, 3.2
.05 Evaluate and retire information	ST 4.7, 7.1	4.3	CM SP 2.2; GP 3.2

Build, Acquire & Implement (BAI)	ITIL	ISO/IEC20000-1:2011	CMMI-SVC
09 Manage Assets			
.01 Identify and record current assets	ST 4.3	6.4, 9.1	SSD SP 2.2; CM; (WP SP 2.3)
.02 Manage critical assets	ST 4.3 (4.2)	6.4, 9.1	CM; WMC SP 1.4
.03 Manage the asset lifecycle	ST 4.3 (4.2); (SS 4.3)	(6.4), 9.1, (9.2)	SD GP 2.6, CM, WMC SG 1
.04 Optimize asset costs	ST 4.3 (4.2); (SS 4.3)	(6.4), 9.1, (9.2)	GP 2.3; CAM; (SD)
.05 Manage licenses	ST 4.3	6.4, 9.1	(GP 2.3)
10 Manage Configuration			
.01 Establish and maintain a configuration model	ST 4.3	9.1	CM SG 1
.02 Establish and maintain a configuration repository and baseline	ST 4.3	9.1	CM SP 1.3
.03 Maintain and control configuration items	ST 4.3 (4.2)	9.1	GP 2.6; CM SG 2
.04 Produce status and configuration reports	ST 4.3	9.1	CM SG 3
.05 Verify and review integrity of the configuration repository	ST 4.3	9.1	CM; GP 2.9

Deliver, Service & Support (DSS)	ITL	ISO/IEC20000-1:2011	CMMI-SVC
01 Manage Operations			
.01 Perform operational procedures	SO 6.4, 6.5		SD SP 3.2
.02 Manage outsourced IT services	SD 4.8	7.2	SAM
.03 Monitor IT infrastructure	SO 4.1, 6.4, 6.5; (SD 4.4, 4.5)	6.3	SD SP 3.3
.04 Manage the environment	SO 6.4, 6.5		SD SP 3.3; GP 2.8
.05 Manage facilities	SO 6.4, 6.5		SD SG 3; GP 2.8
02 Manage Service Requests & Incidents			
.01 Define incident and service request classification schemes	SO 4.2, 4.3 (SD 4.3)	8.1	IRP SP 1.2
.02 Record, classify and priorities request and incident	SO 4.2, 4.3, 6.3; SD 4.7 (4.3)	6.3, 8.1	IRP SP 2.1
.03 Verify, approve and fulfill service requests	SO 4.3, 6.4, 6.6	8.1	IRP SG2; SD SP 3.1
.04 Investigate, diagnose and allocate incidents	SO 4.2, 6.4, 6.6, (4.4)	8.1 (8.2)	IRP SG 2
.05 Resolve and recover from Incidents	SO 4.2, 6.4, 6.6	8.1	IRP SPs 2.3, 2.4, 2.5
.06 Close service request and incidents	SO 4.2, 4.3, 6.3	8.1	IRP SP 2.4
.07 Track status and produce reports	SO 4.2, 4.3, 6.3	8.1	IRP SPs 2.4, 2.5, 3.2; GP 2.8
03 Manage Problems			
.01 Identify and classify problems	SO 4.4	8.2	IRP SPs 2.1, 2.2
.02 Investigate and diagnose problems	SO 4.4, 6.4, 6.6	8.2	IRP SPs 2.2, 3.1
.03 Raise known errors	SO 4.4, 6.4, 6.6	8.2	IRP SG 3; GPs 2.7, 2.10
.04 Resolve and close problems	SO 4.4, 6.4, 6.6; (ST 4.2)	8.2 (9.2)	IRP SPs 2.3, 2.4
.05 Perform proactive problem management	SD 4.4; SO 4.4	6.3, 8.2	IRP SG 3

Deliver, Service & Support (DSS)	ITIL	ISO/IEC20000-1:2011	CMMI-SVC
04 Manage Continuity			
.01 Define the business continuity policy, objectives and scope	SD 4.6	6.3	SCON SPs 1.1, 1.2, 2.1; GP 2.1
.02 Maintain a continuity strategy	SD 4.6	6.3	GG 2
.03 Develop and implement a business continuity response	SD 4.6 (4.7)	6.3 (6.6)	SCON
.04 Exercise, test and review the BCP	SD 4.6	6.3	SCON SG 3
.05 Review, maintain and improve the continuity plan	SD 4.6 (4.3; SS 4.5)	6.3 (6.1, 7.1)	SCON SG2; GP 3.2
.06 Conduct continuity plan training	SD 4.6	6.3	SCON SPs 2.2, 2.3
.07 Manage backup arrangements	SD 4.6 (SO 6.4, 6.5)	6.3	SCON SP 2.1
.08 Conduct post-resumption review	SD 4.6	6.3	SCON SP 3.3
05 Manage Security Services (ISO/IEC 27001)			
.01 Protect against malware	SD 4.7	6.6	SM SP 1.1
.02 Manage network and connectivity security	SD 4.7; SO 6.4; (ST 4.3)	6.6 (9.1)	SM SPs 2.1, 2.2
.03 Manage endpoint security	SD 4.7; SO 6.4	6.6	SM SP 1.4
.04 Manage user identity and logical access	SD 4.5 (SD 4.4, 4.7)	6.3, 6.6	SM SP 2.1
.05 Manage physical access to IT assets	SD 4.7; SO 6.5	6.6	SM SP 2.1
.06 Manage sensitive documents and output devices	SD 4.7; SO 6.5	4.3, 6.6	SM SP 2.1; CM SG2
.07 Monitor the infrastructure for security-related events	SO 4.2; SD 4.7	6.6 (8.1)	SM SP 2.2
06 Manage Business Process Controls			
.01 Align control activities embedded in business processes with enterprise object (SS)			GPs 2.2, 3.1; IWM SP 1.1
.02 Control the processing of information	SD 4.7 (4.4; SO 4.5)	6.6	SM SP 1.1; (GP 2.6)
.03 Manage roles, responsibilities, access privileges and levels of authority	SD 4.4, 4.7; SO 4.5	6.6	SM SP 2.2; GP 2.3
.04 Manage errors and exceptions	SD 4.4, 4.7; SO 4.5	6.6	SM SP 2.2
.05 Ensure traceability of information events and accountabilities	SD 4.4, 4.7; SO 4.5	6.6	SM SP 2.2
.06 Secure information assets	SD 4.7; ST 4.7	4.3, 6.6	SM SP 2.2; GP 2.6

Monitor, Evaluate & Assess (MEA)	ITL	ISO/IEC20000-1:2011	CMMI-SVC
01 Monitor, Evaluate & Assess Performance & Conformance			
.01 Establish a monitoring approach	SO 6.4, 6.5, CSI (SD 4.5)	4.5, 6.2	GPs 2.2, 2.8
.02 Set performance and conformance targets	SO 6.4, 6.5; (SD 4.3, 4.5)	6.2	CAM SG 1; MA SP 2.4
.03 Collect and process performance and conformance data	CSI 4.1, 5.4, 5.5, 5.7	6.2	CAM SG 2; MA SP 2.4
.04 Analyze and report performance	CSI 4.1, 5.4, 5.5, 5.7	6.2	CAM SG 2; MA SP 2.4
.05 Ensure the implementation of corrective actions	ST 4.2; CSI 4.1	5.0, 9.2	IRP SG 2; SD SPs 3.2, 3.3
02 Monitor, Evaluate & Assess the System of Internal Control			
.01 Monitor internal controls	(SS, CSI)	4.5.4	GP 2.8; CAM SG 2; (MA)
.02 Review business process controls effectiveness	(SS, CSI)	4.5.4	OPF SG 1; GPs 2.8, 3.2
.03 Perform control self-assessments	(SS, CSI)	4.5.4, 4.5.5, 6.2	PPQA, OPF SP 1.2
.04 Identify and report control deficiencies	(SS, CSI)	4.5.4	OPF SP 1.2; GP 2.10
.05 Ensure that assurance providers are independent and qualified	(SS, CSI)	4.5.4	PPQA; GP 2.5
.06 Plan assurance initiatives	(SS, CSI)	4.5.4	PPQA; GP 2.2
.07 Scope assurance initiatives	(SS, CSI)	4.5.4, 6.2	GPs 2.2, 2.9; PPQA
.08 Execute assurance initiatives	(SS, CSI)	4.5.4, 6.2	PPQA; GP 2.9
03 Monitor, Evaluate & Assess Compliance with External Requirements			
.01 Identify external compliance requirements	(SS, CSI)	4.1, 4.5, 6.5, 6.6	SSD SG 1; (SD SP 1.1)
.02 Optimize response to external requirements	(SS, CSI)	4.1	SD SP 3.1; GP 3.2
.03 Confirm external compliance	(SS, CSI)	4.1	SSD SP 3.4; GP 2.8
.04 Obtain assurance of external compliance	(SS, CSI)	4.5.4	GP 2.9

ITG RESOURCES

IT Governance Ltd sources, creates and delivers products and services to meet the real-world, evolving IT governance needs of today's organisations, directors, managers and practitioners.

The IT Governance website (*www.itgovernance.co.uk*) is the international one-stop-shop for corporate and IT governance information, advice, guidance, books, tools, training and consultancy. On the website you will find the following pages related to the subject matter of this book:

www.itgovernance.co.uk/iso20000.aspx

www.itgovernance.co.uk/itil.aspx

www.itgovernance.co.uk/cobit.aspx

Publishing Services

IT Governance Publishing (ITGP) is the world's leading IT-GRC publishing imprint that is wholly owned by IT Governance Ltd.

With books and tools covering all IT governance, risk and compliance frameworks, we are the publisher of choice for authors and distributors alike, producing unique and practical publications of the highest quality, in the latest formats available, which readers will find invaluable.

www.itgovernancepublishing.co.uk is the website dedicated to ITGP. Other titles published by ITGP that may be of interest include:

- It's All About Relationships: What ITIL doesn't tell you
  www.itgovernance.co.uk/shop/p-1359.aspx

- The Definitive Guide to IT Service Metrics
  www.itgovernance.co.uk/shop/p-1167.aspx

- ITIL Lifecycle Essentials
  www.itgovernance.co.uk/shop/p-1285.aspx

We also offer a range of off-the-shelf toolkits that give comprehensive, customisable documents to help users create the specific documentation they need to properly implement a management system or standard. Written by experienced practitioners and based on the latest best practice, ITGP toolkits can save months of work for organisations working towards compliance with a given standard.

Toolkits that may be of interest include:

- ITSM, ITIL® & ISO/IEC 20000 Implementation Toolkit
  www.itgovernance.co.uk/shop/p-872.aspx

- IT Governance Control Framework Implementation Toolkit
  www.itgovernance.co.uk/shop/p-1305.aspx

- ISO/IEC 20000 Documentation Toolkit
  www.itgovernance.co.uk/shop/p-632.aspx

Books and tools published by IT Governance Publishing (ITGP) are available from all business booksellers and the following websites:

www.itgovernance.eu   *www.itgovernanceusa.com*
www.itgovernancesa.co.za   *www.itgovernance.asia*

Training Services

IT Governance offers an extensive portfolio of training courses designed to educate information security, IT governance, risk management and compliance professionals. Our classroom and online training programmes will help you develop the skills required to deliver best practice and compliance to your organisation. They will also enhance your career by providing you with industry standard certifications and increased peer recognition. Our range of courses offer a structured learning path from foundation to advanced level in the key topics of information security, IT governance, business continuity and service management.

ISO/IEC 20000 is the first international standard for IT service management and has been developed to reflect the best practice guidance contained within the ITIL framework. Our ISO20000 Foundation and Practitioner training courses are designed to provide delegates with a comprehensive introduction and guide to the implementation of an ISO20000 management system and an industry recognised qualification awarded by APMG International.

We also have a unique ITIL Foundation (2 day) training course designed to provide delegates with the knowledge and skills required to pass the EXIN ITIL Foundation examination at the very first attempt. This classroom course has been specifically designed to ensure delegates acquire the ITIL Foundation certificate at the lowest cost and with the least time away from the office.

Full details of all IT Governance training courses can be found at *www.itgovernance.co.uk/training.aspx*.

Professional Services and Consultancy

Our expert ITSM consultants can help you to focus on what is really important in service management, highlighting both the relationships that matter and the results that you can influence. The outcome of adopting our recommended management good practice will be process improvements that lead to higher ROI.

We show you how to identify and document process lifecycles in a way that is central to ITSM. Consultancy advice, mentoring and coaching will result in you wasting less time and effort on things that ultimately do not matter. You will also learn through engagement with our consultants and trainers how to consider the effects of your behaviours on those you are connected to, and work productively to influence their decisions and actions.

For more information about consultancy from IT Governance Ltd, see: *www.itgovernance.co.uk/consulting.aspx*.

Newsletter

You can stay up to date with the latest developments across the whole spectrum of IT governance subject matter, including risk management, information security, ITIL and IT service management, project governance, compliance and so much more, by subscribing to our newsletter.

Simply visit our subscription centre and select your preferences:

www.itgovernance.co.uk/newsletter.aspx.

EU for product safety is Stephen Evans, The Mill Enterprise Hub, Stagreenan, Drogheda, Co. Louth, A92 CD3D, Ireland. (servicecentre@itgovernance.eu)

www.ingramcontent.com/pod-product-compliance
Lightning Source LLC
Chambersburg PA
CBHW071133050326
40690CB00008B/1455